BETJEMAN'S LINCOLN ᴬᴸ

edited by Michael Richardson

Marden Hill Press

May 2006

Betjeman's Lincolnshire

a tribute
to celebrate the centenary of the birth
of

John Betjeman
1906 – 1984

by

the Lincolnshire Branch of the Betjeman Society

published in May 2006 by Marden Hill Press
Brickyard House, East Keal, Spilsby, Lincolnshire PE23 4HA

ISBN Hardback   09538078-2-7
Softback   09538078-3-5

Typeset and printed by Cupit Print
The Ropewalk, 23 Louth Road, Horncastle, Lincolnshire LN9 5ED

Contents

Sir John Betjeman

Foreword

by Philippa Davies
Founder and Vice-President of the Betjeman Society

Oh! for the British Isles. What a marvellous collection of counties, each one having its distinct character and variety of towns, villages and hamlets. Have you ever wondered at the comparative lack of repetition of place names, established long before the days of computers and word checks? Broadly speaking, being surrounded as it is by the river Humber to the north, the Wash to the south, the sea to the east and the river Trent and A1 to the west, Lincolnshire is self-contained. Vikings, trains and personalities have arrived and retreated. We all need reasons to pull us off the fast lane of a motorway to start exploring. Nothing could act more like a magnet to visiting Lincolnshire than this scholarly collection of essays by the Lincolnshire Branch of the Betjeman Society. Of course it is also exciting to find out more about Betjeman's favourite places and people.

When the Betjeman Society began in 1988 we foresaw neither a large membership list nor the formation of branches. We merely considered it our duty to organise meetings for members who we thought could travel from all over the country to London, Canterbury, the Home Counties and perhaps to Cornwall and Oxford. How thoughtless! How short sighted! Membership has grown and Branches have formed thanks to imaginative and energetic groups of members. All the Branches are set in their own convenient locality and all are distinctly different. With the centenary of Sir John's birth in sight, the Council of the Betjeman Society threw out a challenge to Branches to celebrate. Lincolnshire took on that challenge and have produced this fascinating book. It is a tour de force. Hours of research, interview and editing have gone into its production. The essays, poetry and pictures are a very fine collection. It is an outstanding example of satisfying teamwork.

Bevis Hillier in his book *New Fame, New Love* and Candida Lycett Green in the books of her father's letters have thrown the county of Lincolnshire into focus. With the details and divergences contained therein they have introduced us to a most wholesome background. Now, together with *Betjeman's Lincolnshire,* the county has the attention it deserves.

Betjeman loved the county of his mother's side of the family and of his favourite poet, the Lord of landscape, Tennyson. It was also home to some of his greatest friends. Most of his regular visits to the county were associated with all of these. He laughed at the place names, one seen near Boston for example: To Old Bolingbroke and Mavis Enderby (underneath which some joker added 'a son'). He sniffed the air and smelt cabbages. He explored and visited all the churches. Enquiringly he leads us to undiscovered ends and corners of interest. He seems to give us licence and confidence to digress. Some are cul de sacs, others are welcome diversions that surprisingly link.

The Purey-Cust family were good Lincolnshire stock and are related to Reverend Robert LLoyd who became first Chairman of the Canterbury Branch of the Betjeman Society. Did anyone other than Peggy Purey-Cust ever earn a generous obituary in The Times having done so little save for having a poem written about her, I wonder? Once I went to a wedding in Lincoln and having a very short time between the service and reception nipped into the Cathedral. A helpful guide told me "whatever you do don't miss the Imp". Recently I visited Rothwell, Northants, and there the kind organist, who showed us round the church, said how proud they were of their Lincoln Imp. Prior to Henry VIII Rothwell had been under the Bishop of Lincoln.

This book is like a good jigsaw. The corners are firmly in their places and the edges defined. Thankfully the writers have left some work for us to do. They have unearthed pages of new information but there are still some pieces which can be turned, tested, fitted or temptingly left for us to find.

I will end my words and leave you to start this book with Jill Rundle's words:

"I'm sure we've been on JB ground with past and future all around."

Congratulations, one and all.

Philippa Davies   February 2006

Introduction

Ghost of Sir John, please take this book,
And read it in a shady nook.
 It shows a county you hold dear,
Our loved and lovely Lincolnshire
Within its pages you will find
Those you might well recall to mind.
There's Henry Thorold and Jack Yates
With other friends from other dates.
For, from the mists of time you must
Remember Peggy Purey-Cust.
Your first love, Peggy, yes, she's here;
Her family came from Lincolnshire.
Old churches were beloved by you,
You'll find them here, please take a pew.
There's countryside of fen and wold,
And Louth and Lincoln to behold.
And stations, trains, close to your heart,
Alas, from most we've had to part.
But if you have enjoyed your look
At all the treasures in this book
Please grant the readers, far and near,
A passport into Lincolnshire.

Jill Rundle

"Ah Lincolnshire, a lovely county"

by Michael Thomas

The above words were spoken by Sir John Betjeman to a 'Lincolnshire Echo' reporter who had tracked him down to Cornwall in 1972 to interview and congratulate him on his appointment as Poet Laureate. [1]

This book of essays aims to give the reader a general picture of Lincolnshire and to explain what it was that attracted Betjeman to the county and to enthuse about it. There are misconceptions about the county which we wish to dispel.

The idea of writing a book about Betjeman's love of Lincolnshire was first suggested by Rodney Lines, a local W.E.A. tutor, when I was talking to him after one of his lectures on Betjeman's poetry and prose at Spilsby. After all, books had been published entitled *"Betjeman's Cornwall"*, *"Betjeman's London"* and *"Betjeman Country"*, but there was nothing about Lincolnshire.

It so happened that the Betjeman Society was then asking its members how the hundredth anniversary of his birth should be celebrated. The Lincolnshire Branch members decided to produce this book to celebrate Betjeman's love of the county. The writers who come from different walks of life were either born in the county or have lived and worked here for a long time. Two or three are 'yellowbellies'. This is a term used to describe someone born and bred in the fens and thought by some to derive from a derogatory term referring to the warty or crested newt, plentiful in the fens.

Various aspects of Betjeman's visits to the county are described: churches, people that he met and stayed with, a consideration of his Lincolnshire poetry and prose, the societies which he helped to form and which he addressed, the city of Lincoln, the market town of Louth, and his means of travel. Betjeman and Tennyson, both poets laureate, are considered in parallel. There is also an explanation of the geological structure which has given the county such varied and beautiful landscapes which particularly influenced Tennyson when writing his poetry. Poetry in a Betjemanesque style is also included.

We know that Betjeman travelled by train and then was driven by car to places of interest. As I write I can see across the field from my window the now closed line which ran from Peterborough to Louth. Betjeman travelled on this line in 1953, which he spoke about in an address to the Lincolnshire Old Churches Trust. The 'Louth Advertiser' reported it as follows:

> *"Lincolnshire appealed to him (Betjeman) because of the extent of its skyline which was so vast. He referred to his journey to Louth from Peterborough on a slow train and saw evidence of that every time he looked at it .....*[2]

Many people regard the county as being flat and uninteresting, and because much of it is fenland it must therefore be damp and dismal as well. However, this is not so. As George Crabbe wrote:

> *" ...... bog, marsh and fen*
> *are only poor to undiscerning men."* [3]

Even Dickens regarded the county as dismal and dreary. He described Lady Dedlock's country place in 'Bleak House' as follows:

"The waters are out in Lincolnshire. The adjacent low-lying ground, for half a mile in breadth, is a stagnant river .... and a surface punctured all day long, with falling rain ...The deer looking soaked, leave quagmires where they pass. ..... The vases on the stone terrace .... catch the rain all day; and the heavy drops fall drip, drip, drip. Therefore my Lady Dedlock .... has left it (the place) to the rain, and the crows and the rabbits and the deer."[4]

Happily, this nineteenth century perception is no longer in vogue. As we know, Betjeman was very discerning, seeing beauty in landscapes, whether flat or not, and in buildings, particularly churches. Many people are surprised when told that the East Coast main railway line in England reaches its highest point of 345 feet above sea level at Stoke summit, six miles south of Grantham.

Lincolnshire is neither wet nor dreary for it is one of the driest parts of England. Whilst it is true that the fens in the south and the marshland along the eastern coastline are flat, they nevertheless have a beauty of their own. Charles Kingsley described the fens as having:

"A beauty as of the sea, of boundless expanse and freedom. Overhead the arch of heaven spreads more ample than elsewhere, as over the open sea and that vastness gave and still gives, such cloudbanks, such sunrises, such sunsets as can be seen nowhere else within these isles." [5]

The sunsets are dramatic, with an array of colours ranging from an angry red to pastel shades of blue and orange stretching out across the sky.

Alfred Tennyson, a true native of Lincolnshire, loved the open views across the marshland with church towers and farmsteads outlined in the background, and beyond them the restless sea.

"Calm and still light on yon great plain
That sweeps with all its autumn bowers
And crowded farms and lessening towers
To mingle with the bounding main." [6]

The Tennyson family spent a number of holidays on the coast at Mablethorpe and Skegness. Alfred remembered these holidays years later when he wrote *The Last Tournament*:

"as the crest of some low arching wave
Heard in dead of night along that table shore
Drops flat and after the great waters break,
Whitening for half a league, and thin themselves,
Far over sands marbled with moon and cloud,
From less and less to nothing." [7]

He was born in the rectory at Somersby in the wolds, a place that has not changed since he left it in 1837 at the age of 28. His father was rector of Somersby and the neighbouring tiny village of Bag Enderby; both are situated in beautiful countryside.

Tennyson was Betjeman's hero. He admired his originality of form, command of rhythm, descriptive powers and the melodious flow of words. It was not surprising therefore that Betjeman was present when the Tennyson Society was formed in Lincoln in 1959. On occasions such as this he would praise the Lincolnshire countryside as he did two years later when he made a recording for the BBC at Gunby Hall, between Spilsby and Skegness. He introduced that broadcast by saying:

"Lincolnshire is like a separate country. It is off most main roads, a wide rolling landscape of silvery church towers, villages of old red brick with groves of beech and ash and lime outlined against enormous skies" [8]

He was again in Lincoln as a speaker at the 'Lincolnshire Past Present and Future' conference in 1963 that led to the formation of the Lincolnshire Association (for the Arts and Heritage).

Leading personalities at the Lincoln conference in December 1963 – right to left: Canon Peter Binnall, Mr. Jack Yates, Capt. Jeremy Elwes, Lord Ancaster, Mr. John Betjeman, Miss Kay Gardner

His address at that conference once more reflected his love of the county:

"I stayed with my friend Jack Yates in Westgate, Louth. It was a lovely clear morning, pale, sharp early winter, late autumn sun. My panelled bedroom ... looked down the curve of Westgate, and I could see in that sharp winter morning sunlight the different browns and reds and pale biscuits of the brick which is such a feature of Lincolnshire; dark red for the 17th century and rather brighter reds for later periods until you get to the yellow brick of the Regency. And I saw the curve of these houses .... arching round the winter trees and that spire of Louth which

13

was sharp in the winter sunlight, superbly proportioned. You will notice always in Lincolnshire, in village and town, where there is an old church tower and a road leading to it, the road curves round so that you see two sides of the tower." [9]

His visits to Lincoln for the founding of the Lincolnshire Association and the Tennyson Society, and to Louth for the founding of the Lincolnshire Old Churches Trust were not the only reasons for his many visits to the county. Family connections going back to Victorian and Edwardian times were another, so he came to Spalding to look up his ancestry on his mother's side.

Mabel Bessie Dawson, his mother, was the daughter of James Dawson whose family were styled 'Builders and Contractors' and traded in the town from the early part of the nineteenth century until the start of the twentieth. By 1905 there was no mention in the county directories (Whites or Kellys) of the existence of the Dawsons' family business and Betjeman may have wondered if the firm had gone bankrupt. However, James Dawson had not actually gone into the business, but had moved to London where he became an artificial flower maker.

Hearsay, from two current Spalding residents, suggests that John Betjeman's father and his mother Mabel, who was born in Islington, visited the Spalding area taking the young Betjeman with them. This seems a reasonable supposition as Mabel would, almost certainly, have wished to see her father's home town and meet relatives. There is a local story that the young John played in the vicarage garden at Pinchbeck, a village near Spalding. But there is no evidence of substance for this.

In Bevis Hillier's *'A Life in Pictures'* there is a photograph of Betjeman as a young boy clutching his teddy bear and above him, looking through the window, an aunt called Elsie Avril [10]. However she was not his aunt, just a family friend! She was a violinist and Betjeman remembered this in a letter to her in 1968 when he wrote a poem which had this line:

"All the airs that you had played!" [11]

It is said that she played at some time in the Skegness Pier Orchestra which gave concerts from the 1890's into the 1930's. In a programme for August 16th 1908, it is stated that 'item 3. will be "Serenade Espagnole" by Betjemann.[12] This was Gilbert Betjemann, who was a violinist, composer and conductor and a cousin of Betjeman's grandfather.

Between 1926 and 1928 Noel Blakiston, a university friend of Betjeman, invited him to stay at his father's rectory at Kirkby-on-Bain, five miles south of Horncastle. It was from here that church crawling in Lincolnshire began. Around them was a wealth of churches to visit, many built in medieval times, and situated in beautiful countryside. The market town of Horncastle was the Roman town of Banovallum. In the market place Henry Sellwood's house once stood. He was the father of Emily who married Alfred Tennyson in 1850. Unfortunately this house has now been demolished and Woolworth's have built, insensitively, one of their stores on the site which is totally out of character with the rest of this Georgian market town. Fortunately, Betjeman saw the house before this act of vandalism.

Sellwood House, Horncastle in 1959.

Later on he visited Grasby, a village between Brigg and Caistor in North Lincolnshire, to see the church where Charles Tennyson Turner, brother of Alfred, had been the incumbent. Charles, too, was a skilful poet but, unlike Alfred, confined himself to writing sonnets. His *Collected Sonnets: Old and New* of 1880 contained 340 examples. Betjeman and Sir Charles Tennyson selected one hundred of these and published them in 1960. [13]

A further visit to Kirkby-on-Bain was made in 1933 by which time Blakiston had married Georgina Russell, the distinguished author. It is interesting to note that Cyril Connolly also stayed with him, but whether his visits coincided with Betjeman's is not known. Other places that Betjeman visited in the 1930's and in the early post-war years were the Vanbrugh-designed castle at Grimsthorpe,

Grimsthorpe Castle, Vanbrugh's north front

Ayscoughfee Hall in Spalding, Spilsby, Stamford, Grantham, Woodhall Spa, Sleaford, Louth and of course Lincoln, with its wonderful cathedral. He was particularly taken by St. Hugh's chapel at the Diocesan House which the precentor had asked him to look at in 1968:

> *"I saw the familiar and distinguished Bodley and Garnier doorway and entrance corridor, but I had no idea I was in for so splendid soaring and awe-inspiring interior."* He thought that *"The proper thing to do with the chapel is to clean it up and then leave it as it is."* [14]

After the second world war Betjeman resumed his editorship of the *Shell Guides.* He appointed Jack Yates, his great friend from university days, a native of Louth, and Henry Thorold, chaplain and housemaster at Lancing College, whose family seat was at Marston, to write the Lincolnshire guide. Over a period of three years Yates and Thorold visited the whole county, including every church. On a number of these occasions they were accompanied by Betjeman and John Piper, the artist. Piper drew sketches and took photographs which were to appear in the Lincolnshire Shell Guide and also in books by Henry Thorold. The sketches appear in *Church Poems.* The Lincolnshire guide was published in 1965 and Betjeman was so pleased with the result that he wrote to Piper:

> *"Lincs is certainly the customer's money's worth .... It is far the best of the Shell Guides..... We have got Pevsner on the run."* [15]

Later, in 1981, he wrote to Thorold:

> *"Last week I took up your Lincolnshire Guide...... ... and read it as though it was a thriller"* [16]

However there is a mistake in the Guide for there is an entry for Moorsby, a place which does not exist. Apparently the entry should have been for Moorhouses, a hamlet near New Bolingbroke. The mistake was not noticed until the work was complete but Betjeman said *"Leave it in, no-one will ever question it."* [17]

Gunby Hall, as mentioned previously, was where Betjeman interviewed. Lady Diana Montgomery Massingberd, who was ninety, in a programme *"I Remember."* [18] Her nephew, Hugh Massingberd, in a letter to me, writes:

> *"Unfortunately none of the family were present, and as the disagreeable housekeeper, then ruling the roost at Gunby, failed even to offer Betjeman and the B.B.C. crew so much as a cup of tea by way of hospitality, it cannot be said to have been much of a success. I fear that interviewer and subject didn't really hit it off. My great aunt, to her shame, rather regarded Betjeman as a writer of doggerel; and for his part Betjeman was not frightfully fascinated by the late 19th century revival of English Music (with a Hey-Nonny-No etc.) which was all she really wanted to witter on about."* [19]

After the interview Lady Diana told the Grimsby Evening Telegraph Reporter:

> *"Mr Betjeman hid a microphone under a cushion. He thought I did not know it was there but, of course I did."* [20]

Gunby Hall, built in 1700, of red brick with stone dressings

Bells ring out through much of Betjeman's poetry. When staying in Louth he would hear the ring of eight at St James' church which has a tenor bell weighing thirty-one hundredweight. In two of his Lincolnshire poems, bells are featured:

"And out of the dark, with a roar and a swell,
Swung, hollowly thundering Speckleby bell."

A Lincolnshire Tale[21]

"Now when the bells for Eucharist
Sound in the market square"

House of Rest [22]

Undoubtedly churches were the great magnet which drew Betjeman to the county on so many occasions. In 1946 he had written:

"Doing a church crawl in the marsh here and in the wolds. This county is
an unspoilt Sussex only with better churches. Keep it dark!" [23]

During his visits he was taken by Jack Yates and Henry Thorold to see most of the fine medieval churches. Boston is well known for its 'Stump'. At 288 feet it is the tallest medieval tower in the country, taller than Lincoln cathedral's central tower or Grantham's spire, and only a few feet lower than that of Louth. The top part is an octagonal lantern tower which stands out as a landmark for shipping and can be seen for miles across the fens. Louth's spire rises to 300 feet and Grantham's, the first of the great English spires built between 1250 and 1300, almost as high at 284 feet. Small, unregarded churches and chapels were also visited. The little brick church of Goltho was used as an American 'New England' church in the filming for television of *Moll Flanders*. Non-conformist chapels such as those in Louth and Legbourne were not ignored, and one of the tiniest churches of all, in a beautiful wolds valley at Oxholme was also visited.

We have included an article by the late Jack Yates which he wrote for *Lincolnshire Life* in autumn 1962.[24] It is entitled 'The Buildings of Louth' and in it he describes the market hall as surmounted by a gay little clock tower. When Betjeman looked at it he praised the building and compared the clock tower to a Venetian campanile -"Venice in Louth".

"It is useless to pretend that I enjoy myself abroad" Betjeman wrote in a letter to Patrick Balfour.[25] To Edward James he said "Isn't abroad awful".[26] This may sound surprising when one considers that he travelled to many countries around the world ranging from the Faroe Islands and Europe to Australia (twice) and the United States. Although he generally enjoyed these visits he preferred the great variety of our countryside, its churches and country houses, its history, its way of life and the security that he felt in places that he knew and loved.

Lincolnshire was one of those places.

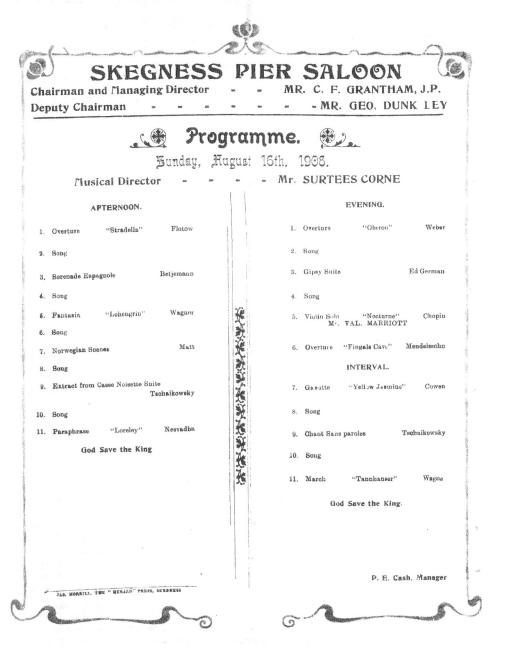

SKEGNESS PIER SALOON

Chairman and Managing Director - -   MR. C. F. GRANTHAM, J.P.

Deputy Chairman - - - - - - - MR. GEO. DUNK LEY

Programme.

Sunday, August 16th, 1908.

Musical Director - - - - Mr. SURTEES CORNE

AFTERNOON.			
1.	Overture	"Stradella"	Flotow
2.	Song		
3.	Serenade Espagnole		Betjemann
4.	Song		
5.	Fantasia	"Lohengrin"	Wagner
6.	Song		
7.	Norwegian Scenes		Matt
8.	Song		
9.	Extract from Casse Noisette Suite		Tschaikowsky
10.	Song		
11.	Paraphrase	"Loreley"	Nesvadba

God Save the King

EVENING.			
1.	Overture	"Oberon"	Weber
2.	Song		
3.	Gipsy Suite		Ed German
4.	Song		
5.	Violin Solo	"Nocturne"	Chopin
	Mr. VAL. MARRIOTT		
6.	Overture	"Fingals Cave"	Mendelssohn
INTERVAL.			
7.	Gavotte	"Yellow Jasmine"	Cowen
8.	Song		
9.	Chant Sans paroles		Tschaikowsky
10.	Song		
11.	March	"Tannhauser"	Wagne

God Save the King.

P. E. Cash, Manager

JAS. MORRILL, THE "HERALD" PRESS, SKEGNESS

Skegness Pier Saloon. Concert programme for Sunday 16th August 1908
These concerts were held each Sunday throughout the summer season

Betjeman's Lincolnshire Poetry & Prose

by Rodney Lines

Lincolnshire, after Cornwall, was Betjeman's next favourite maritime county. What was it that drew him there? Friends, clearly; his love of Tennyson, 'that lord of landscape'; the fact that his mother's side of the family all hailed from the Spalding area of Lincolnshire; above all, the churches. His ideal church, he had once said, would be part Cornish, part Lincolnshire -'Bagby St Petroc' - which, together with the unmistakable county place-names and some unforgettable personalities, all come together in the first poem he composed about Lincolnshire, *A Lincolnshire Tale*.[1] Published just after the end of World War II, it reflects that part of the Wolds he knew so well when he stayed with his Magdalen friend Noel Blakiston at his father's rectory in Kirkby-on-Bain, near Horncastle. Kirkby, indeed, is the first word of the poem, though all the other place-names, authentic Lincolnshire as they seem, are fictitious, especially Sparrowby, with its little dig at John Sparrow, Warden of All Souls College, Oxford, who had made some disparaging comments about Betjeman's poetry. In fact, the whole poem is humorous in a macabre sort of way, which he signals by the choice of hendecasyllables and the use of aa, bb rhyme. It's not really possible to be serious with eleven beats in a line, and it is an ideal form for a dramatic rendering, for the poem performs very well when read aloud. Betjeman's use of the anapaest metre - di,di,dum - keeps the poem moving at a brisk pace, and of course echoes the beat of the pony's feet as he trots along taking the Archdeacon to his fateful meeting.

It is possible to detect Tennysonian echoes in stanzas seven, eight and nine, with references to empty, decaying mansions surrounded by marsh and reed-beds, and this all helps to give the poem its Lincolnshire identity, but where precisely is this place? One clue seems to be in stanza four - *With the Bain on its left bank, the drain on its right* — because this is topographically exact as the River Bain winds its way up to Horncastle, where, a few miles south, is the village of Haltham. Here, the church has a three-decker pulpit. But it also has a roof, which Betjeman's church does not. How about Goltho then, an isolated redundant church near Wragby, set in a large, empty park, and chosen as an illustration by John Piper? But this too has a roof, and it doesn't have a three-decker pulpit.

Perhaps the best candidate is the splendid Georgian church of St Peter and St Paul at Langton-by-Spilsby, where we have the high panelled pews and sign-painter's beasts in their fight for the Crown, and above all, a magnificent three-decker pulpit. But it too has a roof, and is nowhere near marsh, fen, river and drain. And as for the scent of dead cabbages, only someone who knew his Lincolnshire well could have put this in, as any autumn visitor to fenland can attest.

The answer, if there is an answer, is that we have an imaginative conflation of places and names to give the poem an authentic Lincolnshire ring, and this really works, for it is a little masterpiece in its own way. And for a final Betjeman tease, don't try to find the roofless church - it doesn't exist, at least, not in Lincolnshire.

The next poem, not in chronological order, *House of Rest*[2], was published first in Punch in 1953 and next in *A Few Late Chrysanthemums*[3] in 1954, in which the opening word *When* is replaced by *Now,* while in stanza six *large grey eyes* becomes *full grey eyes,* a telling alteration. This is a very different poem, though still with an ecclesiastical theme, where once again the stanza form matches the poem's mood. Here we have ab,ab rhyming, with alternating eight and six beats per line, more like a hymn, one might say. Again, we are located somewhere in Lincolnshire, for Lincoln and Woodhall Spa are mentioned, but where exactly it is not possible to say. We are given quite a lot of internal evidence, such as her husband's name was Harry and that he was ordained fifty years ago, but fifty years from when is another matter. We learn also of a *village church and village pond/And ample rectory* and references to sons and daughters imply at least four children, so this might narrow our search down a bit. For instance, the last quotation seems to fit the little village of Roughton, very near Haltham in the Bain valley, where the incumbent was a certain Henry Spurrier, but the facts and the dates don't quite fit, as he was still alive when this poem was written. The question is, however, are we meant to know the old lady's identity, and does it matter? Betjeman himself does not know the late Revd Harry, otherwise he would have known whether he was High or Low or Broad, something Betjeman had an acute ear for.

Like the previous poem, it appears to be a conflation of people and places that Betjeman actually knew, but the real point of the poem lies not in an actual event in time and place, but as a study of loss and loneliness with the anonymity that often comes with old age, especially concerning women, and is a theme that recurs a number of times in Betjeman's poems. For example, we have the anonymous and lonely old lady in *Death in Leamington*[4], the solitary nun in *Felixstowe or The Last of Her Order*[5], the dying alcoholic night-club proprietress in *Sun and Fun*[6], or the moving *Remorse*[7], and many more. Betjeman is drawn to, and sympathises with, this type of person, before whom he feels humility, and quite often guilt, and may reflect actual personal experience. Maybe his own solitariness as a child and his relationship with his mother causes him to empathise thus. The poem externalises inner feelings of the poet, or the quarrel with ourselves, as W.B.Yeats put it, and the struggle between faith and doubt, powerfully brought home in the last-but-one stanza *With sunshine struggling through the mist,* like light shining through darkness. The reader is able to visualise every line and this engages our sympathy. A very moving poem indeed.

A Lincolnshire Church[8], the third poem about Lincolnshire, was published in 1948, and this time reflects an actual and identifiable experience. The setting is St Margaret's church, Huttoft, near the coast, in the area known as the Marshes (as opposed to the Fens or the Wolds), which he visited most likely while staying with another old college friend, Jack Yates, of Louth. A copy of the poem was in any case sent to Yates's mother in gratitude for her hospitality.

As befits a complex poem in which a number of issues are woven together, Betjeman employs no regular stanza form, and scatters rhyme randomly, while using fairly regular octosyllables to keep the pace moving. The opening lines of the poem display its power by the use of assonance and alliteration, with *t* and *th* chiming with *w* and *o* in *Greyly tremendous* the *thunder/Hung over the width of* the *wold,* the backcloth of the natural world against which the poem is set. The poet appears to be in something of a downcast mood: it's going to rain soon, the place looks a scruffy mess *Of telegraph poles and tin,* he's scornful towards the Americanised cigarette-smoking woman listening to cheap music, and the church doesn't look very promising either, badly restored and with a neglected graveyard. The man-made world, in other words, contrasts badly with the beauty of nature portrayed in the opening lines. And yet curiosity (or the need to find shelter soon?) lead him to open the church door.

This is where the whole thing changes. Clearly, the church is beautiful inside, and what is more, it's Anglo-Catholic, very much Betjeman's persuasion. His mood changes, first to reverence at the beauty of nature and also of a man-made building, and an awareness of the value and importance of everything, including the woman *Of the slacks and cigarette* about whom and her surroundings he'd been so dismissive earlier. And then, overcome with guilt, the familiar words of Psalm 51 come to his mind: *"I acknowledge my transgressions/And my sin is ever before me."*

Now for another surprise. He looks up and there's the vicar, only he's not the usual Lincolnshire clergyman - he's an Asian, like Ghandi of the cinema newsreels of the day. A fascinating character, the Revd Theophilus Caleb was vicar of Huttoft from 1943 until his death in 1959. He lies buried alongside his first wife in St Margaret's churchyard.

The poem has a number of themes, all linked. That appearance and reality are two different things, that one shouldn't therefore judge by appearance, that however awful some of the man-made environment may be, it pales into insignificance in the presence of the divine, and in which, as the last four lines of the poem imply, everything ultimately comes together in what can only be a mystery. The rain, too, has come, so that while it is now no longer light and gold outside, it is inside, at least metaphorically, and so the poem has come full circle. The poem is thus an important learning experience in Betjeman's life which impacts powerfully on the reader too, and that is why it can be reckoned as one of his most significant poem

----

Over the years Betjeman wrote a number of articles which included pieces on Lincolnshire, beginning as early as 1933 in *Ghastly Good Taste* with a spoof entry in Kelly's Directory describing an over-restored Victorian church in the fictitious parish of Loathly-Crumpet with Muckby, four miles east of Horncastle[9]. Then there was a paragraph on Louth in 1953, one of his most favourite market towns in all England, in which he inveighed against hideously inappropriate concrete lamp-standards in a town of otherwise mellow brick[10].

In *First and Last Loves* published in 1952 occurs a chapter entitled *Antiquarian Prejudice*[11] dealing with inept attempts to write local history, often on the part of country clergy, of whose efforts he must have seen scores of examples as he visited churches all over England. This time the fictitious parish is Tickleby Tomcat, once again in the Horncastle area, where first the vicar writes about 'the goodly abbot', with terms like 'glebes, messuages and pottages' which he never attempts to explain, and then pads out his unhistorical conjectures with plenty of sentences beginning with the word 'doubtless', over which there is every reason to be doubtful. This is followed by a much more boisterously romantic piece by the brilliantly invented Mr Sussex Tankard who has little time for the vicar's tame style:

"First to the right after Claxby, then sharp left again down a winding lane, and another turn to the right at the fork, and you are in Tickleby Tomcat. There's something of a good old Lincolnshire ring about the name Tickleby Tomcat, and,

indeed~ the name goes back in various forms till Domesday. Now there is something about picturesque Tickleby that makes it quite possible to imagine Norman barons and monks of old taking (like Abbot Strongitharm, of whom more anon) pleasure in leaning over picturesque Tickleby bridge - or perhaps there was only a ford there then - watching the beautiful Tickold wind its way to the North Sea. The ancient church has a fine double piscina in the porch - on the North side." [12]

As Betjeman dryly remarks, anyone can write like this without actually having been there, providing they can read a map, while *"picturesque" may be used fearlessly to describe anything remote which one has not had time to visit.* And in any case, piscinae are always *"fine"* [13]. It's Betjeman at his satirical best, and wonderful spoof writing, an awful warning to anyone rashly thinking of writing the history of their local parish without undertaking the necessary research in the first place. It's gentle satire, however, written with humility on the part of one who was involved with writing the Shell Guides, where the temptation to romanticise must have been ever present, for he adds *'I say this having fallen into topographical traps of a like nature myself in the course of writing guide-books.'* [14] However, Betjeman had too perceptive an eye and was fundamentally too honest to write in such a manner, which is why his prose is always so original and refreshing to read. It's good to know that some of the most original and refreshing is set in Lincolnshire.

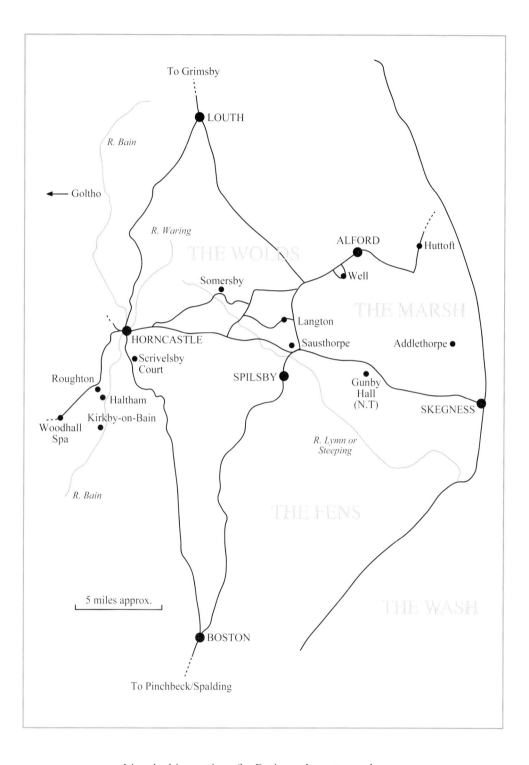

To Grimsby

R. Bain

LOUTH

← Goltho

R. Waring

THE WOLDS

ALFORD

Huttoft

Somersby

Well

THE MARSH

HORNCASTLE

Langton

Sausthorpe

Addlethorpe

Scrivelsby
Court

SPILSBY

Roughton

Gunby
Hall
(N.T)

SKEGNESS

Haltham

Kirkby-on-Bain

Woodhall
Spa

R. Lymn or
Steeping

R. Bain

THE FENS

5 miles approx.

BOSTON

To Pinchbeck/Spalding

THE WASH

Lincolnshire settings for Betjeman's poetry and prose

House of Rest

by David Robinson

John Betjeman first came to Lincolnshire in his early twenties, and stayed at Kirkby-on-Bain with his friend Noel Blakiston, son of the Rector, Canon Blakiston.

Perhaps Betjeman arrived by train to Woodhall Spa, "that half-timbered Camberley among unexpected fir trees."[1] From there to Kirkby it could have been by car or pony and trap across an extensive heather moor.

No doubt the two friends would have explored the area around Kirkby on foot. We can imagine them crossing the wooden footbridge over the disused canalised River Bain, walking along the far bank and back across another footbridge by the lock. Then they would walk along the winding lane with grassy verges and high hedges along the gravel river terrace towards Roughton on its low clay spur. This is still an intimate landscape which impresses itself in one's mind. Halfway between Kirkby and Roughton they would cross the white painted footbridge ,where the old River Bain and the disused canal run side by side, and take the path to Haltham, where they would visit the thirteenth century church.

"With the Bain on its left bank, the drain on the right."

A Lincolnshire Tale[2]

At some time during Betjeman's visits he would have met the Rector of Roughton with Haltham – the Reverend Henry Cecil Marriott Spurrier. He was an Oxford man (Pembroke College) who had held the living since 1913, when he succeeded his father Henry, usually known as Harry, as in the poem *House of Rest*[3]. He lived with his family in a large eight bay rectory, circa 1700, with its own spring-fed pond facing the small greenstone and red brick church of St.Margaret, each within a cricket-ball's throw of each other. Such juxtaposition was clearly still in his mind when Betjeman wrote

"To village church and village pond
And ample rectory."

House of Rest

What of the rest of the poem? Of Harry, of the wedding at Woodhall Spa, of motor-bikes and sons and daughters, and of church bells sounding in the market square? We do not know. So in a typically Betjemanesque way the poem is a conflation of memories and imaginings, teasing and tempting the reader to find a single answer - which there isn't. Yet it leaves the question - who was the rector's widow with whom Betjeman had China tea? Could she have been Canon Blakiston's widow, Mary? And where in that part of Lincolnshire do

".......... the bells for Eucharist
Sound in the market square"

House of Rest

Horncastle? Spilsby? Alford? Boston? Be teased by all means, but don't let it get in the way of enjoying the poem.

Lincoln

by Horace Liberty

There can be no doubt that John Betjeman knew Lincoln well. He described the city as "ancient on the hill and industrial in the valley" [1], and in doing so he used a typically Betjemanesque, journalistic turn-of-phrase which described the city, as he found it, in the middle of the twentieth century.

He highlighted our architectural heritage in *A Pictorial History of English Architecture*, ranking Lincoln alongside other cathedral cities such as Canterbury, Durham and Norwich, where the streets near the cathedrals are "composed of narrow lanes with gabled roofs and no regularity" [2]. Betjeman lists Lincoln Cathedral itself as being an "outstanding example of the Early English style" [3] where "the pointed stone vaulting of the nave is carried to perfection" [4]. However, such fulsome praise needs to be viewed with some caution. Betjeman described a wide range of towns, cities, churches or other buildings, each one being "one of the finest examples of....". But the fact that he described so many places in this way does not detract from the value and uniqueness of the example being considered at the time. It was merely a device that he used to draw the attention of people to an architectural gem in their own locality.

In Lincoln cathedral he was impressed by the way in which:

> *"the masons combined the most elaborate illusions of structure, in the classic form of Purbeck marble shafting, with the most unexpected irregularities of pace and rhythm throughout the eighty-eight years' rebuilding (1192-1280). The vault in the south aisle, for example, breaks up the continuity of its ridge-rib between each bay. Capitals and corbels throughout have the exquisite formalized foliage known as stiff-leaf."* [5].

> *"The Angel Choir takes its name from the thirty angels in the spandrels of the arcade. Yet, even here the flowers and leaves are dominant – oak, vine maple, ranunculus and water lily, carved now with the complete naturalism familiar from St Francis' 'Canticle of the Sun'. Following the introduction from France, via Westminster Abbey, of bar tracery, the clerestory windows show in the separate surfaces of their double tracery the dissolution of the solid wall into a many-coloured translucence symbolic of Heaven."* [6].

Externally:

> *"Lincoln codified the characteristic proportions of the English cathedral, long and broad and low, where the French would be short and narrow and high. But the English have always compensated by erecting high towers – in the case of Lincoln originally with spires as well."* [7].

In typical Betjeman style, he went on to place the building in a setting – in "the misty atmosphere of the hilltop precinct". Again, typically a landscape described by Betjeman is one that is populated. He considered the people who built the cathedral –

> *"Medieval men were smaller in stature than we are today. They lived in squalid wooden cottages with earth floors. That they should have*

produced such splendid and complete buildings as Lincoln in the Early English style is a source of wonder." [8]

Lincoln Cathedral "an outstanding example of the Early English style".

Although he described aspects of Lincoln cathedral as 'perfection', John Betjeman was not beyond suggesting some improvements to the lighting in the choir. In a letter to Mr Harding (11th October 1938), making some suggestions to the Diocesan Advisory Board about churches at Cherry Willingham, Stainfield and Langton, John Betjeman recorded that he had:

> *"attended a service at the cathedral which was 'very nice' and the Canon read exceedingly well and looks a good humorous character, so I enrolled myself as a Friend for 5/-. The choir sang none too well and had to go through the service afterwards as a punishment. I think the lighting of the choir is too bright and too angular. I am sure lights almost level with the human head and much dimmer would be better. The choir looks small with the present floodlighting and glare. Posts with bulbs under dark shades would be better. All Gothic should be lit from low down. I am sure that you and Mr Comper and I agree."* [9]

Jew's House, Lincoln, a well preserved merchant's house of the late 12th century, admired by John Betjeman in *A Pictorial History of English Architecture*.

On 2nd December 1963, John Betjeman was the keynote speaker at the Lincolnshire Past Present and Future Conference in Lincoln. Although this event took place more than forty years ago, we can look back now and see that it was the start of a process of increased cultural and historical awareness in the city. The press reported at the time that:

> *"It was a bitterly cold day in Lincoln ... it was a Monday morning too. And yet more than 200 of some of the County's leading personalities responded to a call to go along to the Theatre Royal for a complete day to listen and take part in what was probably the most unusual conference they have ever attended."* [10]

Another local paper reported:

> *"The first speaker and the conference's main celebrity, Mr John Betjeman, writer and poet, leading exponent of the arts, and a great lover of Lincolnshire, provided the audience with even more to think about.*

His address was witty, yet objective. 'How to save what is left,' he called it, but he made it clear that he was not concerned with preservation just for the sake of it.

He opened with a tribute to the Theatre Royal. 'What a nice theatre this is,' he commented. He was impressed too with the size of the audience. 'I don't think there is another county where you would get so many people to come on a Monday morning and listen to a lot of speeches on the arts,' he added 'But I can understand why you have come. It is that Lincolnshire is so singularly beautiful and is like a separate country from the rest of England. I would like to see it with its own flag and for passports to be shown to get in.'

Lincolnshire's beauty was in its unobtrusiveness. A tribute to the cathedral - 'it is wonderful' – and a word of praise for the county – 'it gives me great comfort' – preceded a rather close examination by Mr Betjeman of West Gate, Louth, where he had stayed with Mr Jack Yates the previous evening. He described its fine aesthetic and material charm and added 'It only needs a concrete lamp standard to spoil it. It would be absolutely tragic if West Gate was ever destroyed,' he declared.

Lincolnshire has two aspects – the land and the sea. He went on to admire the landscape and commented on the unspoilt grass verges which were a feature of the county's roads. It was the most easily damaged county of all and unfortunately people outside it thought it was infinitely expendable, but it wasn't.

Mr Betjeman detailed the places he had visited and what he had liked most. Almost everywhere in the county there was something of charm and artistic merit.

He obviously enjoyed himself by reading out the names of a list of villages, some of which he said were quite remarkable. The names were part of Lincolnshire's charm, he said.

About shops, Mr Betjeman suggested that the trend was to return to the habit of buying from market stalls in open squares. This was his interpretation of modern architecture in the contemporary development schemes. Large glass windows were used on the ground floor and the firms had no use for the upper floors – 'groundfloor stone and vulgarity above' was how he described the policy of a national chain of supermarkets who were building stores everywhere. The firm itself could not be blamed. It had to be remembered that 1963 was the age of the housewife but as we were mostly nomadic people now, he urged that such shops be built away from towns and force people to shop American style.

Pleading for the past and the future to be reconciled he said the biggest enemy was money in relation to development. Concluding, he declared ' Here in Lincolnshire we have started a new revolution. The things we say today must be seriously considered'." [11]

John Betjeman's friend, Jack Yates, also spoke at the conference. However, his comments were not received quite so well by the press:

"Mr Jack Yates, of Louth, discussed old buildings and spoke of the dangers of them getting into the wrong people's hands. But I think he could have chosen his words a little more carefully when, after mentioning that farmers buying large areas of land were not interested in the house in its centre, he said: 'They let hens get into the drawing room and pigs in the kitchen and you see three cows coming down the main staircase abreast, just like any hunt ball." [12]

As a direct result of the 1963 conference, the Lincolnshire Association was formed (John Betjeman was an early Vice-President), and this led to the establishment of the Museum of Lincolnshire Life in 1969. Although the conference at Lincoln took place over forty years ago, many of the issues highlighted by John Betjeman then are remarkably topical and relevant today. He spoke of congestion and the homogenisation of the High Street - a subject that has had been much discussed in 2005, following the publication of the NEF report 'Clone Town Britain'. But this was a subject that had concerned John Betjeman for many years. In 1956, he had described the situation:

"Parked cars make it impossible to see the ground floors of any buildings, good or bad, old or new. Chain-store tailors of no taste, and multiple dress shops of still less, and other chain-stores with their black glass fascias and neon lettering proclaim in their different stridencies that they are making all the old shopping streets of England the same." [13]

Also, in 2005, there have even been suggestions that Lincolnshire should have its own flag. The comments that John Betjeman made in 1963 have a strange resonance, in our city, today.

John Betjeman was tireless in his campaigning for the preservation of our heritage. In this, Lincoln is representative of the many towns and cities in which he tried to save buildings. As he wrote in a letter to Iain Horobin in 1970, this was: *"...an unpaid and exhausting task but essential to my conscience."*[14] Lincoln was also one of the cities featured in Amery and Cruikshank's influential book *'The Rape of Britain'*, to which John Betjeman wrote a foreword. When this book was published, in 1975, Lincoln has already suffered much destructive redevelopment and there were plans for an inner ring road, which threatened to cut across the High Street and sever the medieval hill town from the rest of the city. Eighteenth-century cottages in Sincil Street were also earmarked for redevelopment.

Publication of Amery and Cruikshank's book may have helped to influence public opinion and, following a timely shift in power within the local authority, some of the plans for redevelopment were shelved. But in the fight for the preservation of our cities, even if one battle is won, constant vigilance is needed since there will be another one just round the corner. As John Betjeman warned us:

"If there is some street or old shop in the market square, dock, factory or warehouse, barn or garden wall which you have passed often and taken for granted, do not expect to see it still there next week. Because it is not listed, because it is 'of no historic interest', the bulldozers will be in and part of your background will have gone for ever." [15]

Eighteenth century cottages in Sincil Street, saved from redevelopment in the 1970's

Frank Delaney described *'Betjeman Country'* as a mix of buildings and people, written about "with affection and respect for their place in, and their contribution to, the values of society's continuity . . . who comfort by their very presence."[16] Thankfully, visitors and residents alike can still find much of the Betjemanesque to interest and delight us in the city of Lincoln, if we only have eyes to see it. However, we also have the responsibility to ensure that the aspects of our heritage that John Betjeman admired, are not destroyed, but preserved for the future.

Lincolnshire Landscapes

by Stuart E Crooks

John Betjeman's *A Lincolnshire Tale,* first published in 1945, provides an evocative image of Lincolnshire, with its references to Wolds and Fen, and suggestions too of isolation:

> *"The remoteness was awful, the stillness intense,*
> *of invisible fenland, around and immense ..."* [1]

It also hints at something more, of other, un-named landscapes that might exist elsewhere:

> *"Twas a sinister place, neither fenland nor wold ...".* And the bells of Speckleby
> *"...ring o'er fenland and hill ...".* [2]

conjuring up swelling uplands not so far away.

Betjeman appreciated that there is more to the Lincolnshire landscape than the county's all-pervasive image of endless fen. In *A Lincolnshire Church*, published in 1948, we have a glimpse of another landscape (neither fenland nor wold) in the description of "this green enormous marsh". We know that the subject of the poem is the parish church at Huttoft in the Lincolnshire Outmarsh.

To the outsider Lincolnshire scarcely exists at all. Somehow England's geography is distorted in the popular mind so that the land between the Wash and the Humber, if there is indeed anything between Norfolk and Yorkshire, is '*terra incognita*'. Vaguely, there may be some recognition that there is a zone of flat land somewhere in the vicinity of the Wash.

Though fenland occupies no more than one quarter of Lincolnshire, it has come to symbolise the county, perhaps more strongly than in some neighbouring counties such as Cambridgeshire which have little else. Why this should be is a slight mystery, for the county is in truth highly varied and the major communication routes that pass through Lincolnshire – the Great North Road (the A1), Ermine Street and Barton Street - all tend to follow the higher ground of the limestone and chalk.

The underlying geology on which the county's diverse countryside is founded is quite simple, with rocks of the Jurassic and Cretaceous gently dipping eastwards, the Oolitic Limestone and the chalk standing out as highlands with west-facing scarp slopes, features which run roughly north-to-south. But underlying clays, and superficial glacial sands and boulder clay – all manipulated by the great forces of the Ice Ages – serve to add complexity and local detail which in turn lend the county great variety and character.

Despite the county's fame for potatoes and bulbs, the prevalent landscape is a rather typically English scene with gently undulating scenery, hedged fields and scattered hamlets. Stamford and the villages of the Lincoln Edge or Heath are built of limestone, giving a resemblance to the Cotswolds rather than eastern England. In the eastern half of the county there is a dearth of good building stone, so that the Wolds market towns and villages are mostly of brick. Lincolnshire is one of England's least wooded counties, yet it has – a little known fact – some fine woodlands of national significance. Ancient woodlands with a more or less continuous wooded history since the last Ice Age are widely scattered, but there are three prominent groups worthy of note. On the eastern flank of the Wolds, woods of ash and oak, many with a coppice layer of hazel, are scattered between Louth and Alford. In the Kesteven clay vale there is another group of similar woods with added variety of lime and service. And in central Lincolnshire around Bardney there are the famed Lincolnshire Limewoods where the small-leaved lime, a scarce tree in England, is the dominant species.

The western border of the county is bounded by the north-flowing River Trent with its attendant clay vales and siltlands, a level landscape looking eastwards to the steep scarp of the Lincolnshire Limestone which forms an almost continuous ridge from north to south of this large county, broken only by the gaps at Lincoln (through which flows the modern River Witham) and at Ancaster (formed by an earlier glacial version of the Witham). Any one who claims that Lincolnshire is flat should be walked up the scarp face on the route of Lincoln's Steep Hill. It is no accident that the top of this hill was chosen for the site of the Cathedral. From the top there are commanding views of the Trent Vale and, because of the gentle dip slope to the east, there are fine views of the Cathedral to be had from many parts of mid-Lincolnshire and the Wolds. To the north of Lincoln the limestone ridge (or "Lincoln Edge") is narrow, but to the south it broadens to form the Lincoln Heath. Further south the limestone is dissected by other valleys where it presents the more broken landscape of the old county division of Kesteven. Abutting the limestone to the east is an extensive clay vale, which runs down to the southern fen.

From the limestone the view to the east reveals the long low outline of the Wolds. In reality, once one is among these hills, they seem not so low. Indeed, they take in the highest ground in eastern England south of the Humber, rising to some 550 feet at the highest point near Acre House, Normanby-le-Wold, and include some outstanding landscape features, with a broad rolling upland in the north, with a more dissected area in the south where there are some deep combes. Little of the chalk appears at the surface: most is blanketed by glacial deposits, but here and there fragments of downland survive. Much of the land is given over to extensive arable farms, but large pockets of pasture survive.

The Wolds, looking north to the Bluestone Heath

A prominent chalk ridge in the southern Wolds carries the Bluestone Heath Road, an ancient trackway which runs a good way north. But in the south it follows a more or less east-west internal scarp, south of which the chalk has been stripped by glacial action to reveal the underlying Spilsby Sandstone.

Snipe Dales nature reserve and country park, near Spilsby.

This southern part of the Wolds, stretching to Spilsby, and almost as far as Horncastle, known as the Spilsby Crescent, has its own distinctive character. It is in this part of the Wolds, close under the chalk ridge, that Tennyson was born and grew up, lending the name "Tennyson Country" to this attractive intimate landscape set around Somersby, Bag Enderby and Tetford. Tennyson's poems are full of references to his childhood haunts and the *"Calm and deep peace on this high wold..."* [3]. Here, too, is Tennyson's Brook – several in fact – that join up to drive the mill-wheel at Stockwith Mill.

"I come from haunts of coot and hurn,
I make a sudden sally
And sparkle out among the fern,
To bicker down a valley". [4]

John Betjeman came here, to Somersby, in 1968 for the making of the film *Tennyson: A Beginning and an End.*[5]

To the east of the Wolds lies the Marsh, divided into the Middle Marsh and the Outmarsh. Oddly, there is no "inner" Marsh. The name Marsh is a little misleading as it is – or was until quite recent times – mainly a pastoral landscape of small fields and hedges. Based on a platform cut into the chalk by wave action at a time of much higher relative sea levels, it is a fairly level landscape. The wave action also created a line of chalk cliffs – rather like today's white cliffs of Dover – which has since been eroded, giving the false impression of an eastward-facing scarp. This is the hill which ascends steeply westwards from the market towns of Alford and Louth. Like the other market towns of the Wolds, they are set at the foot of the hill, on the perimeter of the Wolds. The Middle Marsh, running up to the foot of the degraded cliff-line, has a capping layer of boulder clay of glacial origin, giving it a somewhat "lumpy" character, quite different from the flatter Outmarsh and the absolutely flat fen. The surface of the Outmarsh – the strip closest to the sea – is a layer of flat marine deposits.

Between the Wolds and the limestone ridge, and in several of the larger valleys, deposits of sand and gravel give rise to other landscapes, where sandy soils lend a "heathy" character. One of the most extensive of these is the Fen-edge around Woodhall Spa and Kirkby-on-Bain, described by Yates and Thorold in the Lincolnshire Shell Guide as *The heathery, birch and pine landscape"…*[which]… *"give a sudden appearance of Surrey near Bagshot"* [6]. These sands and gravels were spewed out by the putative River Bain – the main tributary of the Witham – flowing from the heart of the Wolds, through Horncastle into the edge of the glacial fenland lake. This heathy district includes special places such as Kirkby Moor and Ostler's Plantation, and the two championship golf-courses of the English Golf Union.

Around Market Rasen and Scunthorpe, and extending into the Isle of Axholme (that isolated division of Lincolnshire lying on the wrong side of the Trent), are areas of blown sand known as the Coversands, which also give rise to heathy landscapes and some fine, but fragmented, grass and heather heaths such as Linwood and Scotton Commons.

Turning now to the last of the chief terrestrial landscapes of Lincolnshire, let us not forget that the south-eastern quarter of the county – the old Holland division – does indeed consist of that *"fenland, around and immense"* [7]. Surrounding the great estuary of the Wash, the fens once formed a vast wetland, drained to provide some of the county's richest farmland. The last large area to be drained, the East Fen, lying between Wainfleet and Stickney, was drained only 200 years ago. Fen is, properly, a watery environment, but the drainage of south Lincolnshire was so thorough that not a vestige remains of the great wetlands that once supplied Londoners with plentiful wildfowl from the ten or more fen decoys. Only the name, and the great cloudscapes, remain, and now the name fen is taken to describe the vast acres of level farmed landscape hedged with ditches and given over to intensive arable production and bulb growing around the principal fenland towns of Boston and Spalding. But not all drained fenland is the same. Look more closely, and one may make the distinction between the silt fen and the peat fen. Also, running around the southern Wash is a slight ridge of raised ground characterised by medieval villages such as Moulton, Whaplode, Holbeach and Sutton, and distinguished by an organic road network. To landward the fen drainage is marked by straight roads and ditches. To seawards, the land has been reclaimed from saltmarsh by building new, and ever larger and higher, sea walls.

Thus we arrive at the last of Lincolnshire's great landscapes – the sea coast. From Trent Falls at Alkborough (where the River Ouse meets the River Trent to form the prodigious estuary of the Humber), to the Norfolk border, close to the outfall of the River Nene in the Wash, is a distance of some 105 miles. Now that Lincolnshire is part of the East Midlands Region, it is worth observing that Lincolnshire possesses the entire regional coast (and a good part of that of the Yorkshire & Humberside Region as well).

The two estuaries, the Humber and the Wash, with their attendant sand and mudflats, and fringing saltmarsh, are landscapes in their own right. Here the rivers carry their load of silt to the sea, giving succour to one of our richest environments – biologically more productive than the best farmland. These great wild places are home to teeming wildfowl and wading birds, fuelling stops on the long migration routes.

High tide on the mud flats and salt marsh near the mouth of the Wash.

Between the two estuaries – from Killingholme to Gibraltar point – there lies a sandy stretch of coastline, known to thousands from holiday trips to Cleethorpes, Mablethorpe and Skegness. The developed holiday coast may have its attractions, but in between the towns there is a lesser-known landscape of sand-dunes, saltmarsh and seashore. The broad dunes and marsh of Donna Nook and Saltfleetby form the largest unbroken section where the gently sloping beaches mean that the sea is generally a long way off. But as one travels southwards the shore narrows and bulges gently into the North Sea, so that between Mablethorpe and Skegness there is no saltmarsh, only a steep beach mostly flanked by concrete sea walls built to protect this vulnerable part of the coast.

South of Skegness the accreting shore broadens once more. Here lies Gibraltar Point, a complex of seashore, saltmarsh, freshwater marsh and dunes on the north-west corner of the Wash. At the apex, where the shore turns sharply south-westwards into the Wash, there is the unusually placed feature of a river outfall – the small un-navigable Steeping River or Wainfleet Haven. This is the outfall of what is known upstream as the River Lymn which carries the tributaries of "Tennyson's Brook" from the Wolds. The accretion of successive sand and shingle ridges has pushed the shoreline eastwards, so that the old coastguard station now has only distant views of the sea. On a clear day there is a view across the mouth of the Wash to the Norfolk coast of Hunstanton and Sandringham, which has the mysterious appearance of a North Sea island, the low land disappearing into the flatlands of the southern Wash.

All of the distinctive landscapes of Lincolnshire can better be understood and appreciated by considering the extra layers of soils, vegetation and human history. Each has its characteristic human settlements and wildlife habitats, moulded by a combination of geology, ecology, climate and land-use history, which together produce that subtle blend that imprints its enduring identity. This big county – the second largest in England and perhaps the least known – has riches and diversity which repay exploration and which justify Betjeman's view that Lincolnshire is a sort of different country, cut off from the mainstream of England, a quality which it shares with his beloved Cornwall.

The shoreline at Gibraltar Point

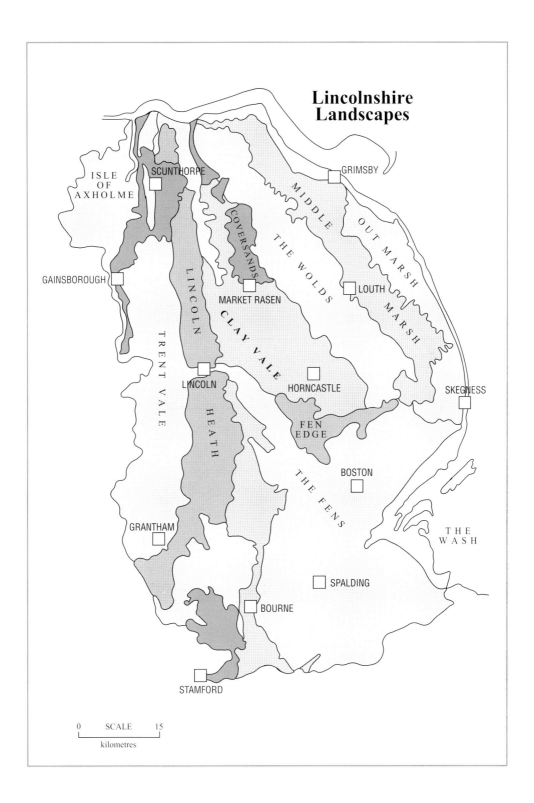

Lincolnshire Landscapes

ISLE OF AXHOLME

SCUNTHORPE

GRIMSBY

COVERSANDS

MIDDLE

OUT MARSH

THE WOLDS

GAINSBOROUGH

LINCOLN

CLAY VALE

MARKET RASEN

LOUTH

MARSH

TRENT VALE

HEATH

LINCOLN

HORNCASTLE

SKEGNESS

FEN EDGE

BOSTON

THE FENS

GRANTHAM

THE WASH

SPALDING

BOURNE

STAMFORD

0   SCALE   15
kilometres

Bust of Alfred (Lord) Tennyson, Poet Laureate

in Somersby church

Betjeman and Tennyson

by Elizabeth Thomas

"Tennyson was the greatest and most melodiously observant nature poet England has ever known."[1]

These were the words of John Betjeman in a radio broadcast of 1950. He also pointed out that it was Tennyson's upbringing in and love of his native county which gave him his earthiness, his understanding of country people and his rather sardonic sense of humour.

Betjeman greatly admired Tennyson's poetry. Some of his poems, such as *The Ballad of The Revenge,* the young Betjeman learned as a child and remembered all his life for the resonance of the words that roll off the tongue and the images that are imprinted on the mind.

Many of Betjeman's visits to Lincolnshire were connected with his interest in Tennyson and he gave enthusiastic talks on his hero's poetry whenever he could. One of his lectures, given in Lincoln on 4th Aug. 1959, opened the celebration of the 150th anniversary of Tennyson's birth.

The following year at the inaugural dinner he was thanked for his help in forming the Tennyson Society and he became a vice president. In 1969 he came to the annual dinner in November to propose a toast to his friend Sir Charles Tennyson, a grandson of the poet, who was celebrating his 90th birthday. Ten years earlier the friends had collaborated in selecting the best sonnets of Lord Tennyson's older brother. *A Hundred Sonnets of Charles Tennyson Turner*, published by Rupert Hart-Davies came out in 1960.[2]

Tennyson's cottage at Mablethorpe, in the 1890's

During 1968 a film was made for the BBC *Tennyson – a beginning and an end.* directed by Julian Jebb. Betjeman and Sir Charles both took part.[3]

Betjeman and Jebb stayed overnight in Louth then went to Golden Sands close to Mablethorpe where the Tennysons had sometimes taken a cottage in summer. Here Betjeman took off his shoes and socks and rolled his trousers up above the ankles. Still carrying his umbrella, furled and still wearing his hat, with his collected poems, presumably Tennyson's tucked under his arm, he crossed the sands where the Tennyson brothers had run, also barefoot, shouting their lines of poetry to the waves and the wind. And I wonder if Betjeman shouted too?

The rest of the filming was done in Somersby, the crew staying at the White Hart in Tetford for ten days, and then at Farringford, Isle of Wight.

Betjeman continued to give his support to the Tennyson Society when possible (though by this time Betjeman was ill) particularly with the appeal, launched in 1980, which led to the purchase of the manuscript of *'In Memoriam'* for the Tennyson Research Centre.

The two Poets Laureate were born almost a century apart, Tennyson on 5th August 1809 and Betjeman on 28th August 1906. They had much in common. Childhood and schooldays were not the happiest for either of them.

Tennyson was born in the rectory at Somersby, a secluded hamlet lying some miles to the south of the market town of Louth and it is little changed today nearly 200 years later. He was the fourth son (the third living) of George Clayton Tennyson and his wife Elizabeth. Dr. Tennyson, who had acquired a degree of Civil Law, was well read and had been to Cambridge but his father, also George, seems to have pressed him into the church for which he had no calling. The Doctor complained constantly of lack of money and the position due to him.

His father (the Somersby children called this grandfather, The Old Man of the Wolds') was neither kind nor just and certainly he favoured his younger son but increased his financial allowance to try to improve matters. Unfortunately the Dr. had grander ideas than he could afford. At some time there were ten servants living with the family including a valet. Elizabeth was affectionate and gentle with a great love of animals but seems not to have been a good manager. It was difficult for her with a large family. Once she was anxiously nursing eight children in bed with measles and was pregnant yet again. There were to be eleven children in all.

The rectory grew ever more crowded and the Dr. took to drink which worsened the seizures he suffered from. The three oldest boys had been having some teaching in the village school and studying classics with their father from an early age but as his health began to break down it was decided to send them away to school. Alfred would join his two older brothers at Louth Grammar School. He was seven years old.

Alfred was fortunate to board at his grandmother's house in Westgate where his kindly aunt Mary Anne Fytch cared for him.

The head of the grammar school was Rev. J. Waite, a relative of the Fytche family. Even allowing for the time he must be seen as a brutal flogger of little boys. One child, according to all sources, was so badly beaten that he was in bed afterwards for weeks. The masters were sarcastic, which to a shy child like Tennyson was nearly as bad as a beating and in such an atmosphere bullying was rife.

His ordeal lasted four years, then he was home. Tennyson would never walk down School Lane again. Later he would say that he had learned little at school. Of the headmaster he said, '1 believe poor old Waite meant well by us." Forgiving indeed.

Betjeman was born in Parliament Hill Mansions in the Highgate Hill area of London. His father ran a prospering cabinet-making business and had a good eye for what would sell. He employed skilled craftsmen and treated them well. There were charabanc outings and some of his senior men were allowed to use his boat on the Norfolk Broads.

He was a smart, upright-looking man, a keen sportsman with gun and rod and he was a good games player. He was also very deaf and used a large ear trumpet. His wife was Mabel Bessie Dawson, whose family origins lay in Lincolnshire. She was pretty, amusing and sociable. She also had social aspirations and very soon the family moved up to 31 West Hill.

It is difficult now to understand the delicate gradations of social standing in a street at that time. Even a few houses further up the street might indicate superiority. At the very top were Georgian houses, in one of which lived the young Betjeman's first love Peggy Purey-Cust. From her possible friendship he was simply frozen out. At another house, after a party he heard himself referred to as a "common little boy". The Betjemans however had holidays in Cornwall which were the envy of other neighbours.

Betjeman's first nanny was a kindly, placid lady, Hannah Wallis, and his first school seemed happy too. There was a bullying incident, probably his first experience, but this took place on his way home.

When he moved to Highgate Junior School the bullies were already there and the headmaster was a ready hand with the cane. The children had to stand round him in a circle and he fired mental arithmetic questions at them. A child who could not answer was shaken until he cried. Perhaps this happened to Betjeman. Like many highly literate people numbers held little interest for him and he was not a good manager of money. Nor was Tennyson at times, though he became better at demanding his dues and Emily managed things well.

One of the masters who did not use the cane was T. S. Eliot and Betjeman showed him a manuscript entitled The Best Poems of John Betjeman. Like Tennyson, he had decided from the earliest age to be a poet.

Later in life Betjeman would say that what he had learnt at school was how to bribe bullies with sweets, lie and show off just enough to not get into trouble.

Of the headmaster, Kelly, at least he stopped boys throwing steel-tipped pen nibs dipped in ink at each others' heads.

By this time Betjeman had a new nurse, Maud. He remained an only child and like many small and lonely children he created his own companion in the shape of Archie, his teddy bear.

Maud was a Calvinist who inculcated the young John with a fear of the fires of hell so that he had nightmares about the devil. Once for some misdemeanour she locked Archie in a cupboard, the unfairness of punishing the innocent one adding to the distress John felt.

Tennyson also met Calvinism in his aunt, Mary Tennyson (Bourne) who told him, "Alfred, whenever I look at you I think of the words Depart from me, ye cursed, into the everlasting fire."[4] Not comfortable words for a boy in his mid-teen years. Perhaps he was able to share them with his siblings and so take the sting from them.

When he was 11, Betjeman went to boarding school. He was happier at the Dragon School though photographs throughout his childhood show a somewhat apprehensive-looking child. He had the chance to act in school plays foreshadowing his TV appearances.

At 14 he went on to Marlborough. Again he hated school. He described the horrors of the bullying on a radio programme and it was always the boys good at games that seemed to be running the school. Betjeman hated team games and sport in an age when both were equated with manliness. His father was impatient with him because he was hopeless with a gun.

However, Betjeman was sharpening his wits now and took his golf clubs to school. He was able sometimes to get out of games and develop a good round of golf instead.

Tennyson had no interest in games either but he was great walker. At 11 Tennyson had left school. When Dr. Tennyson was fit he was a good teacher but he continued to drink. With his father morose or in a towering rage, his oldest brother Frederick at Eton and Charles at Louth for another year, Alfred became the man of the house. Probably this was when the rest of the family began to depend on him.

The Dr. had a fine library and his son read widely; a great range of English literature from Spenser to Byron and Scott, Eastern history, mythology and books of travel. Tennyson was educating himself.

The situation in the rectory grew worse. There were several dogs, a monkey that bit unwary ankles and a pet owl. With such a large brood of children, some passionate and most of them intelligent, there were bound to be clashes.

On one occasion the Dr. threatened to shoot his oldest son and when the gun was removed he threatened to cut his throat instead. There is the famous story of the servant Horlins rushing in, and flinging the horse's harness at his master's feet and telling him to clean it himself. Mrs. Tennyson feared for her safety and told the Old Man of the Wolds that she wanted to leave her husband, taking the younger children with her. It must have been like living through the more melodramatic scenes of *Wuthering Heights*.

Alfred could bear no more and went to Cambridge to join his two older brothers at Trinity College.

"He left Cambridge mutinous against its authorities and negligent of most of its studies." So wrote Peter Levi in his biography of Tennyson. Change the word Cambridge to Oxford and it applies equally to Betjeman.

In his time at Cambridge Tennyson made friendships which would last throughout his life, men who would support and encourage him. His greatest friend, whom he met in his second year was Arthur Hallam. Tennyson and Hallam were invited to join a group known as *The Apostles* who met each week to read papers and talk.

Tennyson enjoyed the companionship and he listened to the argument from behind great clouds of smoke. He had begun to smoke at school and he filled his pipe with a rough shag tobacco that would, of course, be cheaper than a more refined leaf. He lacked the self confidence to enjoy discussion and when it was at last his turn to read and start the evening's talk he was so nervous that he tore up his paper and resigned.

These men remained his friends, they listened to his poetry and indulged him by not criticising. He was becoming spoilt for they were sure that he was destined to become a great poet.

Dr. Tennyson was still in France, so Tennyson took Hallam home to Somersby for a few days before Christmas. Hallam found the informality delightful, and during another visit in 1830 fell in love with Emily Tennyson. In the same year Tennyson's book, *Poems, Chiefly Lyrical,* was published. Hallam unfortunately thought good reviews were coming in too slowly and in 1831 wrote an anonymous piece for a magazine. The following year Christopher North, an influential critic, savaged this piece and went on to give consideration to the poems. Tennyson was furious because he was hurt, both on his own account and Hallam's.

All his life he dreaded criticism and later, when he was married, his wife Emily would hide the less favourable reviews from him. Betjeman too found criticism of his work painful to accept and in his poem *Tregardock* [5] he likened the great sloping slate rocks with their jagged teeth-like steps to "journalism full of hate" and himself as "exposed to ridicule and hate".

After Betjeman became friendly with Mary (Lady) Wilson he wrote to her of the literary world being "malicious and personal" [6] but he advised her to go on writing and publishing. In another letter he wrote "The greatest inhibitor of writing poetry is the thought of anyone else seeing it. Then one also wants it published. What a fix." [7]

In 1925 Betjeman went up to Magdalen College, Oxford. He was to go as a commoner, that is at his father's expense because he had failed 'Responsions' twice. This was an elementary test in Latin and Maths. Again there was the lack of interest in numbers or even money except to worry that he might not have enough.

At Cambridge Tennyson, in spite of his brilliant intellect, would have been unlikely to pass the 'Tripos' exam. He spent the time of his attendance in lectures on mathematics, reading poetry.

At Magdalen Betjeman had another link with the county for the college was built by William de Wayneflete, Bishop of Winchester and chancellor to Henry VI. Betjeman appreciated the fine architecture and the glory of the Wayneflete Tower from which choristers welcome the dawn of May Day. In his old age William did not forget his native village and in 1486 built Magdalen College School at Wainfleet which is just off the A52 between Skegness and Boston.

The college emblem was the Wayneflete Lily and the obvious student joke was that "they toiled not, neither did they spin." Certainly Betjeman did not. He became one of the bright young things of the twenties; it was so easy to drive up to London towards the bright lights. He sought aesthetes and the socially notable and with his wicked sense of fun he entertained them so that he was welcome at country house parties.

Tennyson had a very entertaining manner amongst his friends (though he could be gruff and shy in strange company). He tended to invite himself to stay with them and may at times have outstayed his welcome. He was not averse to accepting financial support, notably from Fitzgerald who later became famous for *The Rubaiyat of Omar Khayyam of Naishapur.*

Betjeman was more likely to offer help to others, though without business sense. Also, when he was living in Cloth Fair, he became a regular and welcome visitor to some of the terminally ill patients in St. Bartholomew's Hospital.

Both men left university without a degree. Betjeman, surprisingly considering his interest, failed Divinity. He went back for an attempt to take a pass degree for which he needed a second language. With wicked perversity he insisted that it should be Welsh, putting the college to the expense of sending for a professor in that language twice a week from Aberystwyth. Did he know that Tennyson and his wife had spent a holiday in Wales and also tried to learn Welsh? It seems the sort of information that Betjeman might have acquired about his hero.

Tennyson went home for the death of his father. His grandfather, the Old Man of the Wolds , had power of attorney and suggested that Alfred might return to Cambridge if he would study for Holy Orders. The poet declined, possibly bearing in mind his father's difficulties as well as his own disinclination.

After this he seems never to have considered seeking any paid employment though he and his brother Charles were the only two in that large family who ever earned a living. Later, Tennyson's poetry paid and, in a radio broadcast, Betjeman pointed out that Tennyson was the last English poet to make a decent living out of poetry.[8]

The years after university were particularly difficult for Tennyson. There was a streak of melancholia in the family. One brother went into an asylum for life and his closest brother, Charles, became dependent on opium. All tended to hypochondria and leaned on Alfred. It was hardly surprising that he often felt ill himself.

Betjeman continued to be a bright young thing and had a furious row with his father because he refused to go into the family firm. He took a series of jobs to earn his living: teaching, journalism and film critic.

Neither man was seen as a satisfactory son-in-law. Having enough money to support a wife mattered. Emily Sellwood had fallen in love with Tennyson and they considered themselves unofficially engaged. Emily was intelligent and well read, and Tennyson enjoyed their correspondence. But their own plans for the future were complicated by the drug problems of his brother Charles.

Charles seemed to have overcome his opium addiction but: was so nervous after his own marriage to Emily's sister that he took the drug again. This made their marriage unhappy and they spent some years apart. Henry Sellwood was not willing to hand over a second daughter into the care of another of the same family and forbade further correspondence. It was years before they met again and Tennyson was forty-one by the time he finally married Emily.

Betjeman was married at twenty-seven to Penelope Chetwode and the marriage was somewhat turbulent at times. Penelope's father was a field marshal (later Lord Chetwode) and her parents were both serious people. Betjeman had a streak of flippancy and irreverence in his style of humour that they must have found difficult to accept.

Tennyson's humour was more laconic. He always called the lake at one house where he lived '**a** muddy pond' and referred to a photograph of himself as 'the dirty monk'.

Betjeman's attraction to women is well documented. He liked wide-apart grey eyes, sturdy limbs and freckles. He also appreciated an independence of mind.

After meeting Tennyson's wife, Emily, Carlyle described her as "a freckly round faced woman ..."and said that she had "wit and sense." Enough sense not to mind, perhaps, when her husband developed a slightly flirtatious manner toward young ladies and was not too stuffy to enjoy having them sit on his knee.

By the 1930's Betjeman was working for the BBC first on radio, then on television where he was a natural performer ready to use new technology. On a radio programme he described Tennyson's readiness to experiment: Thomas Edison had sent someone to record the three most famous voices of the time. Queen Victoria, as befitted royalty, was able, graciously, to decline. Gladstone, as befitted a politician, missed the point and sent a message for someone to read for him. Only Tennyson accepted and read one of his own poems.[9]

Betjeman's great love was architecture, about which he was very knowledgeable. Tennyson was less so but he wrote a poem for the Queen's jubilee which included an appreciation of the Imperial Institute of which Her Majesty laid the foundation stone:

> *Rich in symbol, in ornament*
> *Which may speak to the centuries,*
> *All the centuries after us.*

It was not allowed to do so. Its demolition was planned in 1956 and the Cabinet of the day gave their agreement. This was one of many sweeping changes in the early post war years against which Betjeman fought as a leading advocate for conservation and campaigned on behalf of the Victorian Society.

In 1959, Betjeman made a recording of a selection of his own poems. The record sleeve has a photograph of him by Cecil Beaton, lounging on the stone seat beside the foundation stone. Today only the tower of the Imperial Institute remains.

In 1843, when Robert Southey died, Tennyson possibly hoped for the Laureateship, but it was offered to Wordsworth who, for his presentation to Queen Victoria, borrowed court dress from Samuel Rogers, an elderly poet who collected literary men about him. Then at last, in 1850, the year of his marriage to Emily and publication of *In Memoriam* the position was offered to Tennyson and he was presented in the following year. With country thrift he refused to spend money on clothes that would be rarely worn. He could find none to hire that would fit, so he too borrowed Rogers' court dress.

Tennyson was a big man, over six feet tall and with well developed legs, no doubt from the many miles of walking he had done all his life. Certainly he was a good deal larger than either Rogers or Wordsworth and there was some concern as to the fit. Fortunately he was able to make his bow without disastrously overstraining the seams and wrote to his dear Emily that "... the inexpressibles were not hopelessly tight."[10]

In 1967 Betjeman was tipped to succeed John Masefield as Poet Laureate. Cecil Day Lewis was appointed: Betjeman succeeded him in 1972. For Betjeman, as there had been for Tennyson, there was criticism and suggestions that he was not a good enough poet for the position. As in Tennyson's time, there were letters to the press suggesting that the Laureateship itself was out of date and should be scrapped.

There was positive rejoicing in one quarter. In the Lincolnshire Echo of 11th October 1972 'The Gossiper' was headed 'Poet Laureate with a soft spot for Lincoln', and followed by:

"I can't trace any records of the masses ever breaking out into spontaneous applause at the appointment of a new Poet Laureate, but I feel quite a lot must have done with the news that the laurel has gone to Sir John Betjeman. I did for one." 'Gossiper' added that: "Betjeman had probably done more towards opening the 'inward eye' of people who would otherwise never dream of opening a book of verse, than any other man alive."

The usual question asked of a new Laureate is about the duty of writing poetry to celebrate state occasions. Betjeman knew that it would be inhibiting and indeed these poems are not his best. He pointed out in a radio broadcast that Tennyson had been the only poet who could write for the great occasions citing The Charge of the Light Brigade and Ode on the Death of the Duke of Wellington as examples.

Prince Albert himself wrote to Tennyson saying that writing such poetry was not a condition of being given the honour. Our present Queen also assured Betjeman in the same way, saying that it was not an obligation, but people seem to expect it.

In the months before Tennyson's marriage in 1850 he was as restless as ever and his friend Carlyle remarked that he did nothing but "travel in railways and dine." He was evidently enjoying the latest form of transport and eating well with friends. Some time later he appears to have invested £1,000 in the East Lincolnshire Railways.

When he was still at Cambridge, Tennyson had journeyed to Spain with his dearest friend Arthur Hallam, taking money to rebel forces. On their return via Dublin they travelled on the newly opened line between Liverpool and Manchester. Years later he would say that he had been on the very first train following the official opening by the Duke of Wellington.

However he gave the date as the 20th of September. He may have remembered the date or he may have been indulging in a little poetic licence, as writers are apt to do to improve any tale. Poor Walter Huskisson, an MP for Liverpool and a great supporter of the new railways, had already been fatally injured five days earlier. Despite warnings not to do so, several people descended from the train during a stop for the engine to take on water, and Huskisson was felled by a train on the other track, drawn by Stephenson's Rocket.

Sir Charles Tennyson, in his biography of his famous grandfather, says only that they reached Somersby late in September and Alfred went back to Cambridge later than Hallam.

In the 20th century Tennyson was honoured by having an engine named after him. Lord Tennyson was one of the last steam engines built by British Rail in 1951. The 'Britannia' class pacific no.70032 was in use on the western side of the country, Luton, Penrith and Glasgow being part of the run.

Between 1902 and 1907 the 'Saints' class of engine were built in Swindon. Several of them were named after Tennyson's ladies. *The Lady of the Lake* was no.2902 and *Lady Godiva* no.2904. Tennyson began one of his poems:

> *I waited for the train at Coventry;*
> *I hung with grooms and porters on the bridge,*
> *To watch the three tall spires; and there*
> *I shaped*
> *The city's ancient legend into this;*

It was simply a prelude to the story of the lady's courageous ride through the streets but it showed the dichotomy in Tennyson's mind: modern development and the fascination with ancient legends in his poetry. The last of the 'Saints class' series was no.2910 the *Lady of Shallot.* All these engines were scrapped in 1954.

Betjeman loved travelling by rail; he considered it the most civilised way to move about the country and he enjoyed working out complex cross-country journeys from Bradshaw. Naturally he was a connoisseur of railway architecture but he enthused equally about the great London termini, Huddersfield and Newcastle station buildings and small station halts where the staff still took pride in the flower beds and competed for 'Best Kept Station' of the year.

Many of Betjeman's films were about railways or viewing the country from them and many of his poems involved railway journeys or were inspired by them. '*Middlesex*'[11] begins with an electric train running gaily into a station but is a lament for a lost innocence. The rhythm follows that of the '*Lady of Shallot*' and the name of the fair Elaine is not lightly chosen. There is sardonic humour in calling her a bobby-soxer for Elaine has no part in the young life of her times, no rocking in the aisles; rather her Windsmoor coat would be worn by a vicar's wife from a Barbara Pym novel, up to London for the day to buy the confirmation presents. Both the mirror and the TV screen needed to crack.

As early as 1950 Betjeman had broadcast on Tennyson as a humourist. In particular he pointed to the last lines of 'Enoch Arden' as being part of Tennyson's sardonic wit:

> *And when they buried him the little port*
> *Had seldom seen a costlier funeral.*

Alford station, some ten miles south of Louth, was one of those closed. The street, now home to a small industrial estate, has been renamed with the dry Lincolnshire wit which Betjeman believed informed Tennyson's humour 'Beechings Way'.

Betjeman's own honours from railways came late in his life. In January 1978 he was taken for a splendid train ride around London ending at Charing Cross. There in the hotel he renamed the fine Victorian dining room the *'Betjeman Restaurant'.*

At last, in June 1983, Betjeman was able to name his own engine at St. Pancras Station. By now he was in a wheelchair and it was his last public appearance. The *Sir John Betjeman*, an electric train, after an initial 'special' to Bedford, went west, like Lord Tennyson before him, plying between Euston and Glasgow.

Present as guests on both occasions were Walter Sinkinson and his wife. Sinkinson was a retired railway signalman from Mirfield who had written a book of prayers and other thoughts which Betjeman found a great comfort. Betjeman suffered grave religious doubts: Sinkinson had unswerving faith.

Betjeman had always had a great fear of death and his faith and doubts were evident in his poetry throughout his life. After a short period of worshipping with the Quakers, he turned to The Church of England and remained faithful to it for the rest of his life. It was a blow when his wife became a Roman Catholic.

Tennyson too expressed doubts in his poetry. 'In Memoriam' which he began after the untimely death, in his early twenties, of his dear friend Arthur Hallam being probably the best known. It includes such lines as:

"There lives more faith in honest doubt,
Believe me, than in half the creeds." ... ... and of stretching
"lame hands of faith
To what I feel is Lord of all
And faintly trust the larger hope."

Near the end of his life, Tennyson wrote his famous short poem *'Crossing the Bar'*. The mood is serene but Betjeman in a radio programme said he thought that the words "hope to see my Pilot" rather than something more positive, chimed with his own feelings. He wrote his own six line verse on the same theme and, true to form, he asked for "the bonus of laughter" to see him through.[12]

Watts' statue of Tennyson stands outside the chapter house of Lincoln Cathedral. He was notably short-sighted and Watts has depicted him peering into his hand at some tiny miracle of nature as he used to do. Some Lincolnshire wit dubbed it 'The Disappointed Cabby'. Perhaps the two men are laughing about that together now somewhere.

Tennyson's memorial at Lincoln cathedral

FLOWER IN THE CRANNIED WALL,
I PLUCK YOU OUT OF THE CRANNIES,
I HOLD YOU HERE, ROOT AND ALL, IN MY HAND,
LITTLE FLOWER-BUT IF I COULD UNDERSTAND
WHAT YOU ARE, ROOT AND ALL, AND ALL IN ALL,
I SHOULD KNOW WHAT GOD AND MAN IS.

Lincolnshire Churches

by Clifford Knowles

Lincolnshire possesses in excess of six hundred parish churches, the vast majority of which are ancient. How many of these John Betjeman visited is not known with any degree of certainty. The purpose of this article is to highlight some at least of those which he certainly did visit and others where it is highly likely that he went to see. The intention is not to present a complete catalogue or gazetteer, but rather to be an appetite whetter for a county and its churches which gave Betjeman much pleasure and for which he had a high regard. The locations of some of these Betjemanesque churches are shown on page 58 and photographs of them are on pages 59 to 80.

In *Collins Guide to English Parish Churches,* first published in 1958, Betjeman introduced the section on Lincolnshire as follows:

"This is the second largest county in England and the least appreciated."[1]

There is no doubt, however, that he appreciated it and had a great affection for the county, not least because of his family's roots. His maternal grandfather, James Dawson, was a Spalding builder whose business unfortunately fell into bankruptcy. It was during the late 1920s, when staying with friends in Kirkby-on-Bain, that Betjeman made one of the first of his many visits to the county. A special attraction for him was the quality of its church architecture coupled with its vast skylines. He considered that English architecture depended more on the skyline than any other quality.

A particular favourite place was the town of Louth. He knew it well from his friendship with local bookseller Jack Yates whom he visited about twice a year. During those visits both men, often accompanied by Jack's mother Emily, made expeditions to the surrounding countryside looking at churches.

During 1952, in response to the Archbishop's Commission on Historic Churches, preliminary meetings began in Lincolnshire to consider the establishment of a county trust to raise and distribute funds for the repair of such churches. On 10th October, 1953, the Lincolnshire Old Churches Trust (LOCT) formally came into being with the Earl of Ancaster as its first president. In addition to fund raising, it also aimed to heighten public awareness of the need to maintain its historic churches.

Within a month of its inauguration, on the 4th November 1953 to be precise, the Trust benefited from a meeting in Louth Town Hall addressed by John Betjeman. The meeting was under the auspices of Louth Naturalists, Antiquarian and Literary Society, of which Jack Yates was president. No doubt he was instrumental in obtaining such an eminent speaker. Although Betjeman's subject was 'Louth and Victorian Architecture', he paid special tribute to the parish church of St. James with its wonderful spire (p74), as well as the delightful Gothic structures of Haugham (p68), Raithby (p77), Biscathorpe (p61) and Oxcombe (p76). He also commented that the churches of Holy Trinity and St. Michael in Louth itself looked well from any viewpoint.

Apart from Louth, Lincolnshire contained many other places of interest for Betjeman. Alfred Lord Tennyson was a favourite poet of his, and Betjeman, along with Yates, visited places in the county connected with him. Somersby rectory where Tennyson was born, is faced by its church of St. Margaret with its pretty churchyard containing its famous 15th century cross (p78). Less than a mile to the south-east is the church of St. Margaret, Bag Enderby (p59), where Tennyson's father was also rector. A mile to the east of the latter lies Harrington Hall with its attractive 18th century garden into which Maud was invited. Within its grounds is the estate church of St. Mary (p67), rebuilt by S. S. Teulon in 1854-5.

Not very far away from Somersby, in an exceedingly pretty place where imposing wrought iron gates mark the entrance to the churchyard, is St. Andrew, Ashby Puerorum. Betjeman was fascinated by Lincolnshire place names as evidenced by those he invented for 'A Lincolnshire Tale'. Ashby Puerorum was one of the names which delighted him. "Puerorum" is translated "of the boys" and so called because revenues from the estate once went to the support of the choirboys at Lincoln Cathedral.

In his book *John Betjeman: New Fame, New Love*, Bevis Hillier refers to two Lincolnshire churches which Betjeman visited with Yates and which provided inspiration for poems.[2] The poems were 'A Lincolnshire Tale' (1945) and 'A Lincolnshire Church' (1948). One of the churches, close to Wragby, was Goltho (p65) which is now in the care of the Churches Conservation Trust (CCT), an organisation which Betjeman helped to bring into being under its former name of the Redundant Churches Fund.

The church at Goltho was the illustration drawn by Betjeman's friend John Piper for 'A Lincolnshire Tale' in *Church Poems*[3], published by John Murray in 1981. The poem relates to more than one church and the place names came from Betjeman's fertile imagination.

'A Lincolnshire Church' in the same volume has Piper's drawing of Horsington church,[4] but the poem really concerns St. Margaret's, Huttoft (p69), and its Indian priest, the Reverend Theophilus Caleb. He was rector there from 1943 to 1959 and is buried in the churchyard. St. Margaret's prize possession is its remarkable 14th century font (p70). Nearly five feet high, it is adorned with the Madonna and Child, the Twelve Apostles, angels, and symbols of the Four Evangelists.

Langton-by-Partney (p71) is a small Georgian building approximately two miles as the crow flies north-west of Partney, which Hillier claims "more than any other, tallies with that in the poem"[5]. The poem to which he refers is 'A Lincolnshire Tale'. Dedicated to Saints Peter and Paul, Langton's three decker pulpit, box pews, hatchments, west gallery, wonderful woodwork and 'Prayer Book' atmosphere would have given John Betjeman much pleasure and satisfaction. The church guide claims that Betjeman describes Langton church as:

"one of the most attractive and interesting churches in Lincolnshire
and therefore in England."[6]

It was the church in which Dr. Johnson used to worship when he visited his friend Bennet Langton. The interior looks much the same as it did in Dr. Johnson's day.

Since the year 2003, the Lincolnshire Old Churches Trust has organised an annual church crawl, kindly and most ably led by the Bishop of Lincoln, the Right Reverend Dr. John Saxbee. In 2004 one of the churches visited was St. John the Baptist, Great Carlton (p66), seven miles south-east of Louth. The lime tree avenue approach to the Victorian lychgate and the lovely churchyard delighted Betjeman when he visited with Yates. So too probably did the organ case which, according to the church leaflet, was "decorated in the Bodley style by Canon Sutton of Brant Broughton"[7]. Great Carlton church is claimed to be the only one in Lincolnshire to hold a Lambing Service in springtime. A rather nice bit of Betjemanesque!

George Frederick Bodley (1827-1907) was an architect whose work was much admired by John Betjeman. In the introduction to the Collins Guide he links him with such worthies as Pugin, Street, Butterfield, Pearson, Gilbert Scott and the Seddings. Lincolnshire has a number of churches containing evidence of Bodley's involvement, either on his own account or in partnership with Thomas Garner. The principal works are to be seen at Brant Broughton (p62/63), Corringham (p64), Laughton (p72/73), Nettleham, St. Mary Magdalene in the Bail *(p73/74)* and the Chapel of Edward King House, Lincoln. Of these, St. Helen, Brant Broughton, with its elegant spire which Bodley raised by seven feet, is arguably the most impressive. He, in conjunction with Garner, restored the whole church and gave it a new chancel in 1876. It is one of the finest of Lincolnshire's churches and must have been seen by Betjeman on his travels around the county.

St. Helen, West Keal, is notable for its tall Perpendicular tower, rebuilt after its collapse in 1881, which gives wonderful views across the Fens to Boston Stump. The south porch commands the visitor's attention by reason of its very large and grotesque gargoyles. The latest edition of the Guide to English Parish Churches (1993), revised by the late Nigel Kerr, states:

"Capitals of N. arcade are its greatest glory (p80)*; dragons fight, pigs are chained, foxes steal and women almost burst from their bodices".*[9]

The rector told me that John Betjeman was very fond of West Keal. It is not difficult to see why!

The foreword to Kerr's revision of that guide was written by the late Henry Thorold, squarson of Marston, Lincolnshire and friend of both Betjeman and Yates. The three went on many church expeditions together using the Thorold sixteenth century Marston Hall as their base. A trustee of the Lincolnshire Old Churches Trust from 1970, Henry Thorold succeeded to the chairmanship in 1983, which he held until ill health brought about his resignation in 1998.

A prolific writer, Henry Thorold was joint author of the Shell Guide to Lincolnshire with Jack Yates, both men having been "conned" into it by Betjeman. Thorold also wrote the Shell Guides for Derbyshire, Staffordshire, Nottinghamshire and County Durham, books on cathedrals, abbeys and priories, Lincolnshire churches, Lincolnshire houses and, what is said to be his masterpiece, *Collins Guide to Ruined Abbeys of England, Scotland and Wales.* A true champion of Lincolnshire churches and all that they stood for, he died on 1st February, 2000.

Betjeman visited Henry Thorold at Marston Hall on many occasions and he could hardly have missed exploring the church next door with its lofty 13th century broach spire, Elizabethan tombs and later monuments to the Thorolds (p75).

Less than a mile to the north east of Marston lies Hougham All Saints (p69), a church which appealed to Betjeman by virtue of its setting and its attractive interior. It is known for certain that John Piper also visited it because the church leaflet contains a striking photograph taken by Piper looking through one of the windows. A solitary building close to the River Witham, it has a Norman arcade with a Georgian chancel, a rare Norman-Revival font dated 1662, monuments to Thorold rectors and a high quality restoration by Temple Moore in 1895-6.

Belton House, now in the ownership of the National Trust, lies about six miles to the south-east of Marston. For three hundred years the home of the Brownlow family, it houses within its grounds the most attractive small church of St. Peter and St. Paul (p60) and a large collection of family monuments by the leading sculptors of the day. So much so that the late Harry Cust who was, incidentally, a relative of Peggy Purey-Cust, is alleged to have said that:

"Belton Church was built to the glory of the Brownlows and in memory of God."

Betjeman visited the church not least because of its proximity to Marston and the fact that Henry Thorold was a friend of the Brownlows but also, perhaps, because of the Purey-Cust connection.

Betjeman had a great liking for church bells and, significantly, gave his verse autobiography the title "Summoned by Bells". He described them as:

"reminders of Eternity" and a belfry as having *"the used and admired look of a social club."*[9]

In the Introduction to the Collins Guide (2nd edition, page 29), he refers to the fact that older bells sometimes are inscribed with beautiful lettering. He mentions in particular two Lincolnshire churches, Somerby and South Somercotes (p57). Sadly the latter was declared redundant in 1986, but it is now in the safe hands of the Churches Conservation Trust. Initial letters of these older bells (as in South Somercotes) says Betjeman, have figure decoration which gives the impression of manuscript illumination transposed on metal.[10] He was an admirer of the craftsman's skill, in whatever form, no doubt inherited from his late father.

Some time in the 1960s, a bellringer at North Somercotes was ringing three bells at once - one with each hand and one with his foot! - when two men arrived. They were duly impressed with his dexterity and told him they had just come from South Somercotes where they had admired the bells. Much later the ringer realised that one of the visitors was John Betjeman. Unfortunately we may never know the identity of his companion. Instinct tells me it was probably John Piper, Henry Thorold or Jack Yates, a quartet of church crawlers the like of which may never be equalled or even encountered again! Lincolnshire is extremely fortunate in having had the four as avid supporters of the county and its wonderful churches.

Inevitably this selection of Lincolnshire churches with a Betjeman connection will disappoint some. What about Boston, Gedney, Grantham, Long Sutton, Spalding, Stow and dozens of others besides, all of which might justifiably claim a place? However those chosen do meet criteria set by Betjeman in writing the Collins Guide, that is they all possess atmosphere and aesthetic merit. Perhaps readers will agree and hopefully find similar pleasure from them as John Betjeman did.

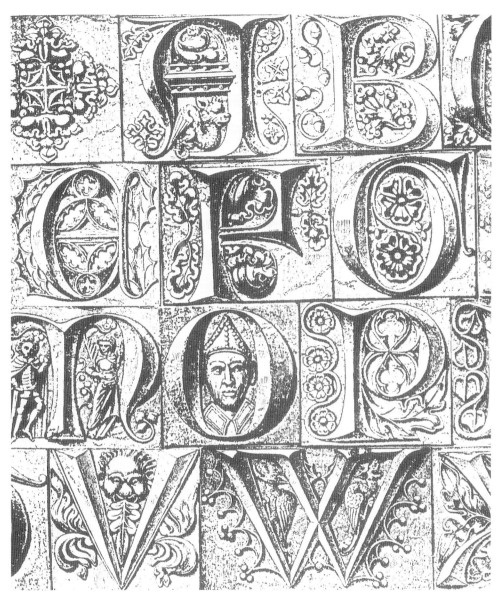

Lettering and stop used on bells cast in 1423
for St Peter's church, South Somercotes

Betjemanesque churches in Lincolnshire

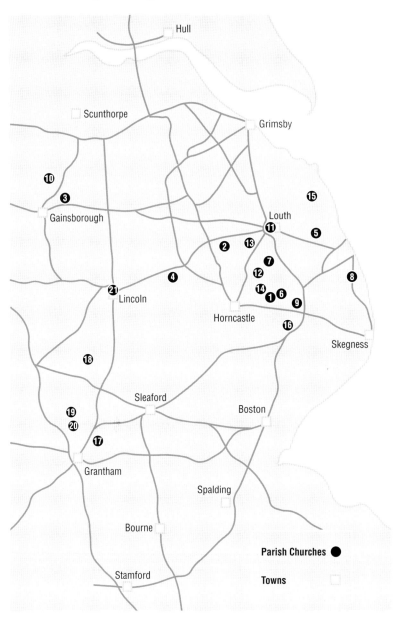

Lindsey

1. Bag Enderby
2. Biscathorpe
3. Corringham
4. Goltho (CCT)
5. Great Carlton
6. Harrington
7. Haugham (CCT)
8. Huttoft
9. Langton by Spilsby
10. Laughton
11. Louth, St James
12. Oxcombe (LOCT)
13. Raithby
14. Somersby
15. South Somercotes (CCT)
16. West Keal

Kesteven

17. Belton
18. Brant Broughton
19. Hougham
20. Marston

Lincoln

21. St. Mary in the Bail

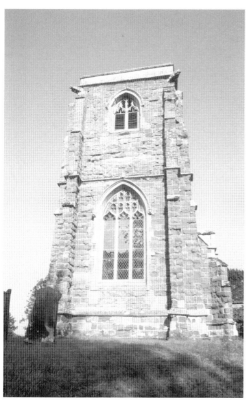

Bag Enderby

Tennyson's father was rector here
from 1806 until his death in 1831.

Belton

Gardens of Belton House and the
walk to church.

(Belton House is the ancestral home
of the Purey-Cust family)

Biscathorpe

The stained glass window behind the altar displays, amongst other features, a sheep reckoned to be modelled on a now extinct Lincolnshire breed

Brant Broughton

Restored by Bodley and Garner, and given a new chancel in 1876

Brant Broughton

The sanctuary

Corringham

Interior restored and decorated
by Bodley, 1884

Goltho

Filmed as a New England
church, in the TV production
of
'Moll Flanders'

Great Carlton

Rebuilt by James Fowler in
1860-61

The only church in Lincolnshire
to hold a lambing service
in springtime.

Detail of the organ case, decorated in the Bodley style
by Canon Sutton of Brant Broughton.

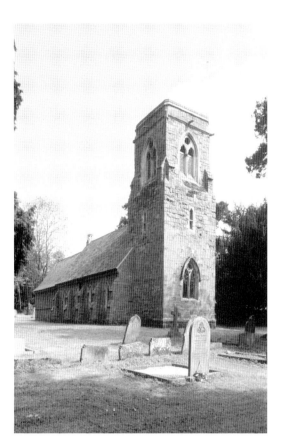

Harrington

The church is beside
Harrington Hall, supposed to
have inspired Tennyson to write
"Come into the garden. Maud"

Haugham

Rebuilt in 1840 as a conscious imitation of St James, Louth,
but in reduced size

Hougham
The church stands grand and solitary by the river Witham

Huttoft
The church described by Betjeman in 'A Lincolnshire Church'.

Huttoft
The font

Langton by Partney

Dr Johnson used to worship here
when he visited his friend Bennet Langton

Looking from the Bennet Langton pews in the west gallery

Laughton
Reredos and rood screen by Bodley

Laughton
A dilapidated medieval church in1896, restored by Bodley

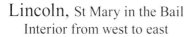

Lincoln, St Mary in the Bail
Interior from west to east

Lincoln, St Mary in the Bail
The high altar

Louth, St James,
Interior view of tower

Marston

The church has a lofty thirteenth century broach spire,
medieval nave and Victorian chancel.
The adjoining Hall is the ancestral home of the Thorolds

Marston
Late 16th century tomb of Sir Anthony Thorold, MP

Oxcombe
Surmounted by an iron coronet of pinnacles
that, according to Jack Yates, gives it 'the appearance of a startled hare'.

Raithby with Hallington

Rebuilt in 1839, in gothic style
with furnishings, like the oil lamp, of the same period.

South Somercotes screen and chancel arch, from east to west

Somersby
South porch and original
15th century churchyard cross

Tennyson was baptised here

Somersby – interior, with Tennyson bust

West Keal
Detail of carving on nave capital in north aisle

A visit to Goltho

by John Ketteringham

Goltho is a remote hamlet not far from Wragby with a church standing alone in a field some distance from the road. To the south west of the church are the earthworks of the deserted village with signs of a fortified hall which is Saxon in origin. Excavations in 1974 revealed several peasant houses.

The church of St George became redundant in 1976 and is now in the care of the Churches Conservation Trust. It is built of brick and is mainly a rebuild of an earlier church. The present building probably dates from about 1530 when the Grantham family bought the Goltho estate. Perhaps because of its proximity to the deserted village which is of considerable archaeological interest the church receives many visitors.

Goltho church from the south

Mr Harry Bruntlett and his wife have been involved with the church for almost eighty years and since its redundancy they have acted as key holders. Many well-known people have called at his house for the church key and on one particular occasion he was not at first favourable impressed with the person making the request.

It turned out that this was in fact the artist John Piper who told him he was meeting Sir John Betjeman at the church. After handing over the key Harry decided to follow on to the church. He was introduced to Sir John whilst John Piper was making the drawing, later included in *Church Poems, illustrated by John Piper* and published in 1981. They had an interesting conversation. Harry said that Sir John appeared to be a true countryman and he was surprised when told that he had been born in London and his formative years were spent in Highgate. During their conversation Sir John commented that the field in which the church stands was very large and Harry told him that the total area was 234 acres and that originally there were around twenty fields. Sir John commented that the hedgerows were highways for birds, small animals and insects and the modern use of machinery meant that hedgerows had to be destroyed with the loss of habitats for these creatures. The conversation moved on to a discussion of changes in agriculture since the Second World War and in particular the introduction of the tractor. This had meant that larger fields were essential so that the tractor could be used to pull corn binders and other large machinery. The actual crops grown had also changed with root crops such as mangolds, swedes and turnips giving way to acre upon acre of yellow oil seed rape.

Whilst Sir John was leaning on a gravestone looking at the rooks' nests in the churchyard trees he remarked "as clever as man is he cannot build a nest like a rook". Sir John had arrived at the church by car and the driver, who was probably Jack Yates, remained in the car with another passenger. Could this other passenger have been Henry Thorold?

Footnote: Henry Lee Bruntlett died on 27 May 2004 shortly after this interview was completed. He was aged 82 and is buried in Goltho churchyard.

Theophilus Caleb

by John Ketteringham

John Betjeman, when staying with his friend Jack Yates at Louth in the late 1940s, visited Huttoft church and, as a result, wrote the poem entitled *A Lincolnshire Church.*

He sent the poem along with his letter of thanks to Mrs Yates, Jack's mother, and later it appeared in *Collected Poems,* which was published in 1958. The reference in the poem to 'an Indian Christian Priest' particularly concerns us here. It seems probable that Betjeman with his friend attended Evensong and were taken aback to find in deepest rural Lincolnshire an Indian priest!

Theophilus Caleb was born in North India in 1878. His father had financed the printing of the first Bible in Hindi and clearly they were a Christian family. After Caleb graduated with a degree in Persian at the University of Allahabad he went to London and was called to the bar.

After his father died Theophilus Caleb was able to pay for training at Chichester Theological College and it was in Chichester that he met his future wife, Annie Elizabeth.

Caleb was ordained in 1907 and served in curacies in the St Albans Diocese before moving to Staffordshire in 1916. He was curate of Caverswall and than moved to Meir, where he remained until 1923. He was appointed vicar of No-man's Heath, Tamworth in 1923 and moved to Lumb in Rossendale in 1926 before moving to Lincolnshire to become vicar of Mareham on the Hill in 1934.

Mareham is and was a small hamlet with most of the parishioners being connected with agriculture in one way or another. The word went round that the new Vicar looked like Gandhi. At that time Gandhi was not receiving a good press because of his civil disobedience campaign. However, it should be realised that, at that time, someone from as near as ten miles away would be regarded as a 'foreigner' in rural Lincolnshire!

Caleb did not always help himself to make friends. The organist at Mareham church sometimes assisted at the Methodist chapel. However, Caleb issued a severe reprimand and told her "she could not expect to go to heaven". He also denounced those 'pleasure seekers' who spent their Sundays at the seaside when they should have been in church. No doubt he didn't realise that many of his flock would be setting off for Mablethorpe after the service. On one occasion he visited the parents of John Timms who owned the local farriers and blacksmith's shop. He noticed a framed print of Robert Burns and was amazed that anyone in Mareham on the Hill should have any knowledge of poetry. John Timms recalls the occasion when the village school children were attending a service in the church and Caleb questioned them on their knowledge of the scriptures. He asked young John what God would want from us. The boy replied 'God would want us to be good'. This annoyed the priest and he shouted at length 'GOOD! GOOD! God wants you to do his work..'

In 1943 Caleb and his wife moved to Huttoft. Sadly, she died within a year and was buried in the Huttoft churchyard on 4th February 1944, aged 73. He lived another 15 years and remarried.

Rev. Caleb in the late 1930's with his wife Elizabeth seated on the left.

Canon John Swaby, who was appointed vicar of nearby Mablethorpe in 1953, says that he preached at Huttoft in 1959 and after the service Caleb said "I am very sorry that I cannot ask you to supper. My wife is ill". Swaby commented that it was plain that Caleb himself was also ill. A few days later Canon Swaby with his wife and daughter decided to revisit the Calebs. They entered the kitchen and found Caleb lying on a couch. He died later that night and was buried in Huttoft churchyard with his first wife..

Caleb was very fond of children and Canon Swaby remembers that his visit with his young daughter made Caleb's last hours very happy. The Rev. Caleb's second marriage was not, however, a happy union and it appears that in his later years things deteriorated badly both at the church and in the rectory. After his death his widow moved away and she too died soon afterwards. To the surprise of the Swaby family she left their daughter Sara a small legacy.

To have an Indian vicar in this area of Lincolnshire was, to say the least, unusual at that time and there is little doubt that he had to endure considerable prejudice. However Caleb was a well-known Anglo Catholic priest and his devout spirituality and pastoral care were much valued by his parishioners.

Kirkstead St Leonard – an early 13th century chantry chapel
just inside the ruins of Kirkstead abbey near Woodhall Spa

Wonderment at Woodhall Spa

(after a Lincolnshire/Shires Branch meeting organised by Horace Liberty on September 15th 2001)

by Jill Rundle

When the news was far from bright, what a day of rare delight
Travelling in modern car, back in time to Woodhall Spa.
Dark green leaves embrace the street, at the Kinema we meet
In the wooded woodland town, quite a jewel in its crown.
Introduction, coffee – good, at the 'Teahouse in the Wood'
Then you guide us, not too far, on a tour of Woodhall Spa.

Break for lunch, once more we meet, Kinema gives us a treat.
On the screen 'Late Flowering Love' – Did J.B. join us from above?
His voice described the tennis fun, in Surrey with Joan Hunter Dunn.
Myfanwy set his heart a-whirl, and so did Thelma's sister Pearl,
While Judy at the poultry farm, romped in the hay and caused alarm.

We could have watched these larks all day, but out we came, the sky was grey.
Still, off we went so we could see, where Woodhall Junction used to be.
Station years from any train, in the thirties once again.
Grassy track, but one can dream, of the golden days of steam.

To distant past to end our day, thirteenth century place to pray.
Stony lanes to Kirkstead church, make our cars give quite a lurch,
Alone in fields yet still held dear, they've had a harvest service here.
Abbey church 'outside the gate', so it escaped its patron's fate.
Raffle prizes in the rain, then back inside the church again,
I read my poem, J.B. style, and hope that it would make him smile.
I think he would have liked this day, "thank you" is what I want to say.

I'm sure we've been on J.B. ground, with past and future all around.

Bayons Manor
a historical note

Bayons Manor, Tealby, near Market Rasen

"Between the years 1836 and 1840, Alfred (Lord) Tennyson's uncle turned Bayons Manor from what had been a small Regency house into an extensive mansion.

This amazing yet splendid building had a great hall, library, reception rooms and a tower. There was an imitation Gothic castellated wall, with two gateways, moat barbican and drawbridge, and a huge ruined keep on a small hill behind the manor.

During the second world war Bayons Manor was taken over by the Army, but after they had vacated it, the building became derelict, falling rapidly into decay. It was finally dynamited in 1965.

Today there is no trace of this stately mansion"

A Guide to Tennyson's Lincolnshire, Skegness Publicity Sevices, 1973

'Is there anybody here from Lincolnshire?'

a memory of John Betjeman in Lincolnshire
by Cressida Jupp and Virginia Wintringham Flew

Our mother, Meg Penning-Rowsell, was born Margaret Wintringham in Grimsby in 1913. She was the youngest child of seven. Her father, John Wintringham, was a member of the Grange and Wintringham law firm in Grimsby, although the main family business was in the timber trade. Mother's uncle, Tom Wintringham, was MP for Louth and when he died on the floor of the House of Commons, his wife, Margaret (known in the family as Auntie Maggie) took over his seat, thus becoming the first English woman M.P.[1]

Our uncle, also Tom Wintringham, was a socialist and a journalist. He fought in the International Brigade in the Spanish Civil War, and as a result of this experience founded the Home Guard in Osterley Park, west London. Our mother left Lincolnshire at about the time she was 18 or 19, but had a very close relationship with her sister, Mrs Elizabeth Neale (always known as 'Jim'), who lived between Brigg and Caistor at Searby Manor Farm. We spent many summer holidays there.

Meg met John Betjeman when we were living near Swindon. She was keen on poetry and went to a lecture he was giving on Tennyson. He asked if anyone in the audience was from Lincolnshire and, once she had identified herself, that was the beginning of a family friendship. The Betjemans were living in Wantage, not far from Swindon, and we used to go over to their house and have rides in the pony trap with Penelope, his wife.

Meg and we, with our brother Edmund, were staying at Searby in the summer of 1949 along with her brother Tom and his children. Tom suddenly died of a heart attack while harvesting. It was a great shock for his sisters and we children and my mother were taken off for a day by John Betjeman to Cleethorpes while the adults sorted things out. We don't remember this but Tom's son Oliver did, writing to Cressida in 2004:

> "An image of Meg that sticks in my mind is the day soon after Tom died at Searby (August 1949). John Betjeman was visiting, and took Meg, me, and you three children out for the day, to take our minds off Tom. We went to Cleethorpes where we romped on the beach. I was 20, you were 7. Meg was 35 and looked so particularly beautiful. I was thrilled. John Betjeman was a hero of mine that I had never expected to meet. The dominant feature of that beach in those days was a vast gasometer at one end. I was inclined to dismiss it & despise it as an ugly eyesore, but John gently suggested that it was worth looking at carefully. He implied that it might be poetic."

And I already knew that he could make poetry out of notices put up by Southern Railway. I have never forgotten that. (C.J.)

Our only real memory of John B. (as we called him) in Lincolnshire was on a picnic, perhaps in 1950 or '51, to Bayons Manor. This was a Victorian large house, deserted and with a completely over-grown garden. We children were both scared and thrilled when Meg and John broke into the manor, climbing into a window into the closed up house, and finding a suit of armour in the hall. They thought it was a great adventure - we thought they would be caught! We believe it is now demolished.

John and our parents were good friends and he used to write letters which were mostly about Lincolnshire, decorated with ink drawings of the landscape: a line for the horizon, a road and two or three telegraph poles sticking up.

This was his view of the county, though we knew Searby as having a steep hill going up the wolds where our farmer uncle Victor Neale had sugar beet fields.

A Lincolnshire landscape by John Betjeman

The Lincolnshire Wintringhams

by Kit Lawie

What more interesting a family could John Betjeman have hoped to encounter than when, at a poetry meeting in Swindon, he posed the question "Is there anybody here from Lincolnshire?"

From that chance meeting in 1949, a long friendship developed between him and Margaret (Meg), her husband Edmund Penning-Rowsell, publisher, journalist and authority on wine, their three young children, and Margaret's relatives back in Lincolnshire.

Margaret and her family were then living at Hinton Parva, on the Berkshire Downs. This was very near to the Betjeman's home in Farnborough as well as their next house at Wantage, which the Betjemans moved into in 1951.

Margaret (Meg) Penning-Rowsell's father, **John Wintringham**, was a lawyer in the 'Grange and Wintringham' law firm in Grimsby. It still survives in many North Lincolnshire towns.

Memorial window to Tom Wintringham MP in the chapel of Little Grimsby Hall.

Her sister, **Elizabeth,** married a Lincolnshire farmer, Victor Neale, and they lived at Searby, near Caistor in the north of the county. As both sisters wrote poetry, it seems there was a double interest that linked her with John Betjeman's own Lincolnshire background. He too, through his mother's childhood connections with Pinchbeck, also visited the county frequently.

Tom Wintringham, (Meg's uncle) and her auntie Maggie (Longbottom)were married in 1903. They were both staunch liberals and they lived in Little Grimsby Hall, just outside Louth, from 1914 until his sudden death in the House of Commons library in August 1921.

Tom had won the Louth parliamentary constituency in June 1920 and after his death Tom's wife, **Margaret**, was the logical choice for Louth Liberals to put forward. She stood for and won the Louth seat in October 1921 and held it until 1924. She became a close friend of Nancy Astor, who said of her "she went about her tasks like a high stepping pony while I stumbled about like a clumsy carthorse".

Margaret Wintringham also had a brother called **Tom** (1898-1949). Early in 1919 he went up to Balliol College, Oxford to read for a shortened course in modern history. In 1920, the year before his liberal uncle became an MP, he joined the Communist Party and in succeeding years he established his reputation as an essayist, pamphleteer, poet and the left's leading commentator on military strategy. He went to Spain in 1936 and fought in the Spanish Civil War. He died on 16[6h] August 1949 after suffering a massive heart attack while helping with the harvest at the Neales' farm at Searby.

Searby Manor, near Brigg
the home of Meg Wintringham's sister, Elizabeth Neale.

Jack Yates

by David Robinson

Jack Theodore Yates was born in Louth on Good Friday 1905 in the vicarage of the 'High Anglican' church of St Michael and All Angels where his father, William Edward, was the priest in charge. Yates' grandfather was a wealthy Yorkshire wool manufacturer and a devout Methodist.

St Michael's church was designed by the famed Louth architect, James Fowler, and was built in 1861-63. Writing in later years, Yates described the polychromatic brick interior as "mysteriously dark, with delicate arcading like a Fra Angelico Annunciation screening the Lady Chapel."(Lincolnshire Life, Autumn 1962). It would seem that this church and the style of worship there were to affect his religious leanings later.

The youngest of four children, he was only ten when his father exchanged the living of St. Michael's for that of the tiny stone and brick church of St Margaret's, Keddington, just to the east of Louth. Nevertheless, the family could still afford to live well, first in Welton Manor at Welton le Wold and then (from 1920) in 'The Mansion' on Westgate in Louth.

After schooling at Radley, Yates went on to read history at Oriel College, Oxford (1924 to 1928), where he liked to be known as Theodore. He practised what he later described as 'masterful inactivity' and only just scraped a degree. Yates forged lasting friendships with Betjeman and others, like AJP Taylor, who moved in the same Oxford circles of aesthetes and 'bon viveurs'.

Going down from Oxford in 1928, Yates ran a preparatory school in Kent for ten years. During that time, Yates came to Louth with Betjeman in the year his father died (1934), when he visited his newly widowed mother.

Yates joined the British Council in 1938 and became Director of the Council's book exhibitions which involved extensive foreign travel, including a large event at Barcelona in 1944 which he later thought was the climacteric, "the peak of the graph of my life"[1]. This was probably when he finally resolved his religious belief and became a Roman Catholic.

Whilst working for the British Council, Yates and Betjeman met again but, by 1948, Yates had become disillusioned with the British Council. He returned to Louth to live with his mother to whom he was deeply devoted, and Betjeman began his often twice yearly visits to stay with him. They were then both in their early forties.

Yates and Betjeman's Lincolnshire jaunts from Louth were sometimes by bus but mostly by car. Jack Yates had always liked fast cars and he became a familiar figure hurtling to meetings in Lincoln in his open-top MG. It is not difficult to imagine them along byways in Tennyson country, around Brocklesby and Great Limber, or going to Betjeman's favourite Woodhall Spa, with Betjeman holding on firmly to his trademark trilby.

In 1960 Betjeman suggested that Yates should take up the task of preparing a Shell Guide to "dear old Lincolnshire" with a mutual friend, the Rev. Henry Thorold. Between 1961 and 1964 Yates and Thorold visited every church in the county and the guide was published in 1965.

Yates was Vice Chairman of the Lincolnshire branch of the Council for the Preservation of Rural England and a founder member of the Louth Civic Trust. In 1968 he advised on and appeared in a half-hour documentary by Anglia TV on "Louth: Change or Decay" in 1968..

Jack Theodore Yates died in 1971, the year before John Betjeman became Poet Laureate. He lies alongside his parents in the churchyard at Keddington.

Mr. J. T. Yates, M.A.

by John Ketteringham

There is no doubt that Henry Thorold deserves remembering as one of Lincolnshire's characters. Indeed, perhaps he should be included in any gallery of this country's personages of the last fifty years.

He maintained the tradition of clergyman-squire at Marston, which had been the home of the Thorold family since the fourteenth century, but, as patron of the living, he would never have dreamt of appointing himself incumbent. He was once described as "having a profile like George III's and a stomach like George IV's... knows Lincolnshire backwards and all the families that ever were, they being to a man his relations."[1]

Henry Thorold

drawn by David Freeman

Henry Croyland Thorold was born on 4 June 1921. His father was Chaplain-General to the armed forces and Henry's lifelong passion for architecture sprang from his father's postings in the cathedrals of Cologne, Chester and Salisbury, in the Royal Military Chapel at Sandhurst and then at St Pauls' Westminster Abbey and Southwark.

After prep. school at Summer Fields, Thorold was educated at Eton and then went up to Christ Church, Oxford before preparing for ordination at Cuddesdon Theological College. He was ordained into the Scottish Episcopal Church during the Second World War, becoming personal chaplain to the Bishop of Brechin. In 1946 he became a naval chaplain, serving in the cruiser *HMS Leander* and then in the depot ship *HMS Forth* where he surprised his fellow officers by taking the ratings to admire the glories of Maltese architecture!

From 1949 to 1968 he was chaplain and also a housemaster at Lancing College where he tended to treat the boys as undergraduates and entertained them (by rota) to lunch or dinner. He took them on outings, by Rolls-Royce, to cathedrals and museums or to Glyndebourne. He was formal in class and very particular about correct pronunciation.

After retirement, he became chaplain at Summer Fields and spent his time between Oxford and Marston until, in 1975, he took up permanent residence at Marston where he remained for the rest of his life.

In 1952 Thorold founded and chaired the Lincolnshire Old Churches Trust, which was the first of the county churches' preservation trusts which raise funds for repairs to ancient parish churches and encourage their continued use. He had a particular gift for inspiring local families to adopt and look after neglected churches which might otherwise become ruinous. Although never an incumbent, he held services in many remote Lincolnshire churches and his declamatory style of preaching with long pauses were famous and kept the congregation on the edge of their seats. He was a great believer in the dignity of worship and was firmly of the 1662 persuasion.

Henry Thorold became a prolific author, writing the Shell guides to Lincolnshire, Durham, Derbyshire, Staffordshire and Nottinghamshire. He also wrote the *Collins Guide to Cathedrals, Abbeys and Priories, Lincolnshire Churches Revisited* and completed a long awaited study of Lincolnshire Houses shortly before his death. The manuscripts for his books were written in longhand with a pad resting on his knee. For his writing he was awarded a Lambeth Degree.

Thorold acquired a splendid 1951 Bentley Mark VI Mulliner in which he visited many churches and country houses in Lincolnshire and further afield. At Marston no television, radio or newspaper was to be found and the house was said to be one of the coldest in Europe as the constant stream of visitors both young and old found to their cost!

The Revd Henry Croyland Thorold, clergyman and antiquary, died on 1st February 2000 aged 76.

The Buildings of Louth

by J.A.Yates
(published in 'Lincolnshire Life', Autumn 1962)

"I went to Louth by train once", said the Diplomat. "It was the dreariest and flattest journey I had made since I motored from Turin to Milan."

"You should have gone there by road from Lincoln" I replied.

It is as you breast the final ridge of the Wolds coming from Lincoln that you get one of the finest views of the spire of Louth; for there you see it at the end of a gently sloping fold in the hills, proudly marking the town which is the centre of the countryside. Or you can see it as you enter the Humber estuary, standing in the distance as a beacon to all that great expanse of marshland that lies between.

It is true that an upstart rival has grown up lately. It is quite a good building of its kind, but it is nevertheless a rival for attention, and it is doubtful if this town of 11.000 people can afford two eye-catchers. This rival is the great white box-like malting factory.

The church spire was finished in 1506 and is built of Ancaster stone, the colour of which changes with every subtle difference in the light. Standard works hold it to be the finest parish church spire in Europe. As it rises some 300 ft., it is a queen of grace. and the flying buttresses from the elaborate pinnacles to the spire seem to make it even more ethereal.

Apart from this great fane of stone, Louth is in general a town glowing with red tiles and red brick. A most pleasing contrast can thus be obtained by looking at the spire from the bottom of the *Wheatsheaf* yard as it rises from a number of high pitched, red-tiled Elizabethan roofs. This is only one of many alley-ways which should be explored for the gentle view of old brickwork which lies behind the more ambitious frontages of the main streets in the centre of the town.

The church itself is rather disappointing. It is an empty shell, heavily restored in late Victorian times with undistinguished windows, encaustic tiles, alabaster reredos, and so on, by the late *James Fowler* of Louth, who altered so many North Lincolnshire churches to his own taste and that of his time. Until the depredations of Henry VIII the church must have been full of altars and adorned with many valuable furnishings and jewels.

There is a little good plate and one important treasure left, which is kept locked in the vestry but may be seen on request. This is the *Sudbury Hutch*, an oak chest carved in the time of Henry VII and bearing a relief portrait of him and his Queen, together with their coat-of-arms. The piece is considered of sufficient importance to merit a full page plate in McQuoid's Standard work, the *Age of Oak*

The east end of the church is good and the east window's magnificent tracery may be admired if you run round to look at it on your way to the Town Hall.

The latter ambitious building whose front looks like an annexe to the Vatican but whose back looks more like a slaughterhouse, contains two large paintings which should not be missed. It is not because they are great works of art, though they do have a look of Lowry about them, but because they carefully show, as if from the Church tower, a view of Louth as it was in 1848. This is well worth studying before going out to see how it has changed.

'Spout Yard' in 1962   *The Town Hall*   *'St Michael's' so inviting*

It has not changed at all in some places as a stroll down *Westgate* will show you. The fine 18th century houses are there, though maybe the occupants are not so fine now. Several of them are used by the Girls' Grammar School and there is a home for the blind, which was built by an Earl of Buckinghamshire in the Gothic style in about 1820. There is a mansion which took on its present aspect at the end of the 17th century and is panelled from top to bottom with heavy bolection moulding. *Thorpe Hall* lies out this way, which is a fine 17th century house built by the Bolles family and said to be haunted by the Green Lady.

On the way back a detour round the Church to look down *Bridge Street* will be a good thing to do, because there is a fine 18th century house facing a good terrace of the same period. From here it would be well to walk up *Upgate*, noting some of the houses on your right and particularly the Mansion House. This is the public library, so you may go in and see the minstrels' gallery (the building was the Assembly Rooms in the 18th and early 19th centuries) and the fine ceiling in the further chamber into which have been screwed a number of particularly vicious pig-trough lights.

On the walls of this library hangs a good collection of local prints and there is a most extraordinary and delicate carving by *Wallis,* a local 19th century artist. Some might think it more skilful than beautiful. There is also a bust of *Newton* said, rather doubtfully, to be by *Roubillac.*

From here it will he pleasureable to walk along *Mercer Row. The King's Head* is a Regency Gothic building which gives you a foretaste of a fascinating house at the other end of the town to be mentioned later. There is a charming old bow window to Goulding's bookshop and if you look up you will see that the upper storeys of the buildings in this street have quite a lot to offer to the lover of architecture.

The *Market Place*, where stands the house (now Parkers) which published Tennyson's 'Poems by Two Brothers', contains some pleasant buildings besides a rather odd brick and slate group, which looks as if it had been transplanted from north Germany. The Market Hall stands behind it and the whole thing is surmounted by a rather gay little clock tower.

Wherever you walk in this charming town you will see houses and buildings of the Georgian and Early Victorian eras, not particularly distinguished, perhaps, but built with good craftmanshipship. This is well shown in the *Cornmarket*, which also contains a rather laughable building, called the *Corn Exchange* adorned by a statue of *Ceres* and many other classical devices. A reproduction of it appeared in the *Illustrated London News* in 1854, but the stone had been cut wrong and the whole front became flaked. Now it is ignominiously lathered in some sort of plaster.

Some good examples of late 18th century brickwork are to be found in the "Engine House" and in Espin's school in Eastgate. The first is to be found between Enginegate and what used to be called *Spout Yard*, and now, with horrible refinement *"Spa Lane"*.

A more interesting building than Espin's school is the late 18th century house nearby called the Priory. This is a white Gothic house of great charm which until lately had some furniture obviously designed for the house. In some ways the rooms

are reminiscent of the Sloane museum with angled corners and interesting archways and alcoves.From here it is not far to the *Riverhead* where are the late 18th century warehouses which once marked the busy terminus of the Louth Navigation Canal.

The Priory in Eastgate

Finally, there is the Betjemanesque frolic which can be made in the town. James Fowler himself provides the polychromatic church of St. Michael and All Angels, mysteriously dark, with delicate arcading like a Fra Angelico Annunciation, screening the Lady Chapel. Holy Trinity Church which, though "Low", has a chancel arch the height of which is accentuated by the low arcading of the nave, with excellent local stone carving of fruit in its capitals.

In this mood we must not neglect the station, which is solidly built like an Elizabethan Manor House; but it is sadly dwarfed by the concrete maltings, and seems to be an epitaph in brick and stone of the decline of the railways.

"Now take me" said the poet "to something that looks like Beaconsfield."
So I took him to *St. Mary's Lane* and it did. As you go outwards from any good
market town it tends to look the same as anywhere else in the United Kingdom, it is
only in its heart that you will find its individuality and that, thank God, Louth has
not yet lost.

Mr J B in Louth
on November 4th 1953

by Jill Rundle

Oh, have you heard the steam trains as they hiss along the track
Illusory reminders of an age that can't come back?
And at the ghostly stations eerie spectres now appear
Guards, passengers and porters, all glide mistily quite near.
Spirits, wraiths and phantoms, who forget they had to die,
They whisper of past memories, of days that have gone by.
To try to recreate one is the purpose of this rhyme,
With help from Mr. Betjeman, we'll journey back in time.
We're off to 1953, ah yes, I think we're here.
Austerity was over and it was a pleasant year.
We'd had the coronation and Sir Winston was a knight,
Everest was climbed in May, a mountain of great height.
Stanley Matthews' medal came when Blackpool took the cup
And Pinza won the Derby with Sir Gordon Richards up.
At last we had the Ashes, Compton scored the winning run,
And sweets came off the ration, which was quite a lot of fun.
And, on one bright November day, a slow train from the south
Brought JB up to Lincolnshire, he'd come to visit Louth.
The Naturalists' Society had invited him to speak
On Louth's Victoriana at their meeting held that week.
And on the way he watched the sky, so vast above the fen
Content to be in Lincolnshire, to visit Louth again.
He noticed Aby station which was kept with skill and care,
With well trimmed hedges, flowers in bloom, a treat to stop and stare.
He also liked Louth station, built a hundred years gone by.
The architecture of that time was pleasing to his eye.
He praised the town's fine houses and the church with lofty spire,
And other local churches, there were many to admire.
In fact, said Mr. Betjeman, this county was the best
To look at and to live in — an improvement on the rest.
His talk was well applauded, he was asked to come again,
And soon JB left Lincolnshire to go home on the train.
Now churches, houses still remain, just as they used to be
And ghostly stations rest in peace, you live in memory.

Betjeman at Sausthorpe

by Kit Lawie

'...... a house with an old garden, worth preserving.
The Queen Anne façade is of plastered brick, masking
an Elizabethan building'

'Lincolnshire: a Shell Guide' (1965)

In 1960, the year of the publication of his blank verse autobiography *'Summoned by Bells*[1]John Betjeman came to stay at the Old Hall in Sausthorpe. He was accompanied by Sir Charles Tennyson: an eighty-one year old grandson of the Victorian poet laureate with a future poet laureate.

Sausthorpe Old Hall

Their hosts, long-time friends of the Tennysons, were William and Anne Kochan, an artistically talented couple who were part of a musical group based at Gunby Hall, the home of Diana (Lady) Montgomery-Massingberd.

William Kochan was the local vet for the Spilsby area from the 1930's until his sudden death in 1970. He had a marvellous singing voice and a most charming manner. His Austrian background may have contributed to both! Whether at a soiree or a difficult calving, his manners were impeccable.

William Kochan,
by Carlos Sanchez

And so it was, in his old grey Rover, that he collected his two guests from the LNER. Firsby station, a branch line destined for closure in the early 1970's and a topic for conversation on the six mile journey back to Sausthorpe.

At dinner Betjeman was, it is said, on top form, trying out some Lincolnshire dialect words and talking of his boyhood visits to the Spalding area with his mother. He remembered playing barefoot in a grassy orchard in Pinchbeck and talked of his grandfather, a Spalding builder who, according to Betjeman, went bankrupt.

After dinner they spent time in the music room which opened onto the garden. A large mural of an Italian lake scene painted by Carlos Sanchez[2] in 1953 particularly took his attention. It still occupies most of the west wall of the room and shows where the Kochans often holidayed.

Italian lake scene, by Carlos Sanchez

Before departing the following day to attend another function with Sir Charles, Betjeman sat for some time in the front porch doing some writing. Margaret Simons, who lived in part of the house at that time, helped with the housework during their visit. She found them both very pleasant and thought John Betjeman quite delightful and charming to her.

As the Kochans had no children of their own, Margaret was treated much as family while she was at the Old Hall. She still has many happy memories of the Kochans and their various interesting visitors.

Benjamin Britten had been one of these guests and so, co-incidentally, the Old Hall had through him another Betjeman connection! For hadn't Britten's librettist, at that time, once been John Betjeman's 'Golden Myfanwy' of the *'black-stockinged legs under navy-blue serge*[3] 'with *'Kant on the handlebars, Marx in the saddlebag'*.[4]

After those early days in Oxford, Myfanwy was to become, of course, Mrs John Piper. Her husband was a visitor to Lincolnshire on many occasions, often in the company of John Betjeman. As co-editors of the Shell Guides, the county became a frequent destination for them both.

Anne Kochan

Postscript

A visitor to Sausthorpe Old Hall in the 1960s, described the way in which the Kochans ran their household – in a style that John Betjeman would have enjoyed!

"Bill Kochan had a big veterinary practice somewhere nearby. They lived in Sausthorpe Old Hall, an Elizabethan near-ruin not far from Aswardby, which they had restored, and Mrs Kochan ran it in Edwardian style, with servants. I was staying with them while arranging and opening an exhibition at the Usher Gallery in Lincoln. I slept in a four-poster bed, had a maid to draw the curtains and wake me with a breakfast tray, and was not expected to go downstairs until all the household chores had been performed! I remember telling friends that a fortnight there would have turned me into a communist.

We were sitting in the drawing room (of course) around an open fire; after evening dinner in the dining room; Mrs Kochan said to Bill "Would you like a cigarette, dear?" Bill said he would. Mrs Kochan rang the bell for the maid (china knob by the chimney breast, clatter of wire in the plaster) who came quickly. "Master would like a cigarette, Mary!" The maid fetched the cigarette packet, put one in Bill's mouth and lit it for him. "Thank you, Mary!"

H.L.

Diana Massingberd playing the viola

Life in nineteenth century Lincolnshire

by Michael Richardson

Almost all of John Betjeman's most enduring Lincolnshire friendships were with people whose families had been brought up in the nineteenth century, living in a relatively remote largely rural county.

For most of that century it was the gentry and an influential middle class of clergy, solicitors and large farmers who ran the county. Only towards the end of the century was there an influx of new wealth from adjoining newly prosperous and mainly industrial areas like Yorkshire and the Midlands.

Among Betjeman's Lincolnshire friends, the ways of life of the Blakistons (clergy), Thorolds (gentry/clergy), Yates (clergy/industrialists), and Wintringhams (solicitors/landowners) were all firmly rooted in the essentially rural society of the county in the nineteenth century.

Betjeman's interest in the past began with an early preoccupation with different styles of mediaeval parish churches and an interest in architecture and art that developed when he was a student at Oxford. There he found books of design for lodges, villas and country mansions that gave him:

> *"a vision of Georgian England that was utterly different from those seen in the big Batsford books. .... These Georgian aquatinted books added to my respect for the landed proprietor, with his gate lodge, park, walled garden, pinetum, icehouse, library, saloon, home farm and spreading stables. I already had a taste for this sort of thing when staying in the homes of my Oxford friends.... ..."*[1]

This contrasted with his awareness of life as it was becoming for many of these friends:

> *"The old house is too big to live in. Servants cannot be got and the rooms are too big to be 'cosy '..... The convenience of your house is solely that of shelter. The telephone (carried by prominent poles that stride down the eighteenth century vista) is ringing all day ..... Your house is too large and unmoveable. You almost want to get rid of it.*
>
> *Here are the two sorts of life. Historically separated from one another by the nineteenth century, the transition period. Preservation of the countryside is but an ineffective compromise. Clotworthy is dead and his sons make motorbikes in the Midlands. The praying of the Nonconformists has been heard and even their own establishments are threatened. The Democrats and the free-thinkers are in. They no longer shout and preach, they are coming up the drive in their motor cars. You are already half a democrat yourself."*[2]

The following account of what Betjeman described as life in the 'transition period' is drawn from a book about *Rural Society and County Government in Nineteenth Century Lincolnshire* that was published in 1979 by the History of Lincolnshire Committee for the Society for Lincolnshire History and Archaeology. It draws heavily on original research by Richard Olney[3] whilst working in the Lincolnshire Archives Office between 1969 and 1975.

Olney's description of rural life in the nineteenth century was not about the Lincolnshire that Betjeman knew when he came to stay with his friends. But Betjeman could still find a wealth of echoes and footprints from the past in the country houses, churches, towns and villages in the county that he came to see with his friends on visits spanning more than forty years:

> *"Glorious Lincolnshire, where ... the Victorian life goes on, unhampered by a convenient railway system and not 'picturesque' enough for the main road motorist."* [4]

Richard Olney's book highlights the lifestyles and roles of landed society (the nobility and squires), the middling sort (agents, doctors, clergymen and farming families) and village life in the county during the 'transition period' of the nineteenth century.

In the following edited text drawn from Olney's book, all of his initial references to nineteenth century families with Betjeman links, like the Brownlows, Custs, Massingberds, Tennysons, Thorolds, Willoughbys and Wintringhams are highlighted in **bold** type.

The County in 1800   *(Chapter I)*

Lincolnshire has never been a county popular with the tourist, but perhaps at no time did it seem so unattractive as in the late 18th century. ... ...Even a town such as Louth, by no means bereft of polite society, could not boast a tolerable inn. .. .... Lincolnshire's human population was in fact less impressive than its vast numbers of sheep. ... ... Flocks grazed on the rich coastal marshes and roamed the partly unenclosed uplands. But the undrained lowlands of Lincolnshire hampered the progress of agriculture just as they hampered the traveller. ... ...

The typical Lincolnshire village of 1800 was neither picturesque nor imposing. The ruinous profile of its parish church reflected the low state of the church in the county, and the parsonage house was likely to be 'of small size and mean construction'. ....

The great landlords were widely scattered and more characteristic of the upland parts of the county than the lowlands. There were concentrations of large squires around Grantham, for instance, and smaller squires around Spilsby. ... ...

A glance at road communications in 1800 serves to bring out both Lincolnshire's isolation and its lack of internal cohesion.... The Great North Road virtually bypassed the county although it did provide Londoners a way to reach Lincoln by way of Newark. ... ...

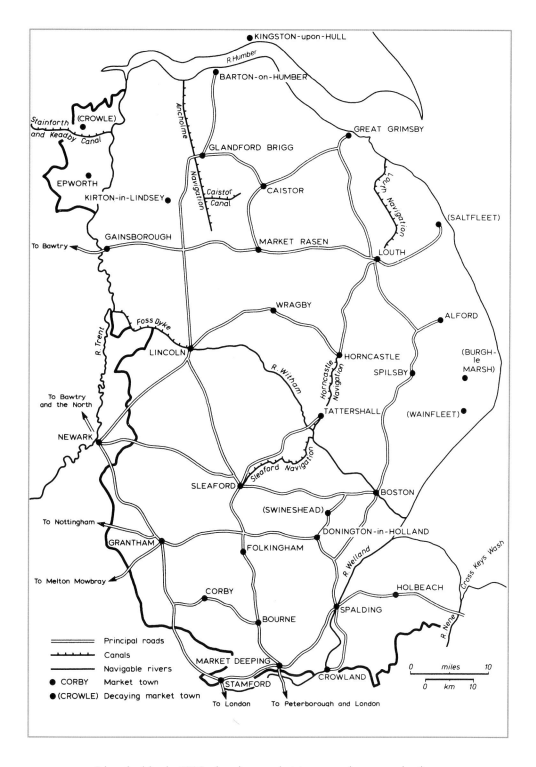

Lincolnshire in 1800, showing market towns and communications

Landed Society   *(Chapter II)*

"In your library there is no sign of the ancestors who founded your family.
Their only memorials are in the church (removed by your grandfather
from the old building at the restoration of 1863)."

John Betjeman, 'An Apostrophe to One of the Landed Gentry'[5]

The Nobility

In 1800 there were an estimated sixty-six-landowners who owned estates of
3,000 acres or more in Lincolnshire. Together they owned about 570,000 acres, or
quarter of the county.

The greatest Lincolnshire magnate was Lord Yarborough with estates
of more than 50,000 acres, almost wholly in the north of the county. The
other great landowners, each with estates of more than 20,000 acres, were the
Duke of Ancaster whose principal estate was at Grimsthorpe near Bourne, Lord
Monson of Burton by Lincoln, **Lord Brownlow** of Belton near Grantham, Sir Gilbert
Heathcote of Rutland and the Chaplin family of Burton and Fulbeck.

In the eighteenth century the houses of Grimsthorpe, Belton and Brocklesby
had all made important alliances within the county, daughters and younger sons
inter-marrying with neighbouring gentry. ... ...After 1810, the Custs made no
important Lincolnshire marriage. ... ...

Although the nobility were the official leaders of the county, their links
*with it were not of the strongest. In the case of the **Custs** (of Belton) and the*
***Willoughbys** (of Grimsthorpe), the acquisition of estates in other counties reduced*
the importance of their Lincolnshire interests and hence the amount of time they
spent in the county. Among the greater nobility the calls of London society and the
demands of court and parliamentary duties militated against any long periods of
rustication. For much of the year houses like Belton and Grimsthorpe were shut up,
their furniture under dust covers and the servants on board wages. ... ... The first
earl Brownlow and the second earl of Yarborough transacted parts of the county
(Lincolnshire) *business from south coast watering places.*

The squires

In his 'Great Landowners of Great britain and Ireland' first published in
1876, John Bateman defined squires as owners of estates between 1,000 and 3,000
acres, reserving the term great landowner for owners of over 3,000 acres. ... ... But
in Lincolnshire the term was much more loosely applied ... ... In Lincolnshire it was
posssible to live as a gentleman on a thousand acres or even less. ... At this level,
however, there was more movement in and out of the gentry class. ... ...

There was only one truly gentrified region in Lincolnshire, and that was
the neighbourhood of Grantham. The combination of pleasant country and
comparatively easy communication with London had long made it a favoured region
for big houses. ... ...

In contrast, the neighbourhood of Spilsby, Spilsbyshire as it was sometimes
called, was a region of small squires. It is a picturesque region of small parishes
in the southern Wolds,.and in the nineteenth century it contained several country
houses whose modest estates did not stretch very far beyond their park palings.
*Here too were to be found ancient families such as the **Langtons** of Langton-by-*
Spilsby as well as more recent arrivals such as the various branches of the

Brackenbury family. Spilsbyshire was not dominated by any strong aristocratic presence, the Willoughbys being non resident on their Lindsey coast estates. ...

The basic qualification for gentry status was of course to have a sizeable house situated within partly ornamental grounds and removed some little distance from the public gaze.

The big house

'This county,' wrote John Britton of Lincolnshire in 1806 'is more noted for its religious than for its civic architecture. Though an extensive district it contains but few mansions of consequence, grandeur or eloquence, and those that are standing are chiefly of modern erection.' A county seat may be defined as a large house standing in its own grounds, owned by a gentleman with a thousand or more acres in the county and occupied either by himself or by a close relative. ... ...

The early years of the century saw a few essays in late Georgian classicism although ... only Normanby survives. Its architect was Sir Robert Smirke, who shortly afterwards designed the assize courts at Lincoln.

The rate of building increased in the 1830's which witnessed the two most adventurous domestic building projects of any period of Lincolnshire's history, Harlaxton and Bayons Manor ...Harlaxton was a grandiose conception, in a flamboyant Elizabethan style of Gregory Gregory, a bachelor squire ... who spoke of his house as his hobby just as his neighbours might speak of hunting, shooting or feasting ... ... Bayons Manor was a Gothic extravaganza, designed by its owner Charles **Tennyson** D'Eyncourt with the assistance of the Lincoln architect William Nicholson. Interestingly enough neither of these landowners began as leading county figures and their mansions, though marvelled at, did not make them so.

It was the early 1840's however, that marked the peak of housebuilding by the gentry, as it may also have marked the peak of their social influence .... The Victorian country house was intended for comfortable family occupation and it was supported by increasingly large numbers of servants. The combination of comfort and ostentation sometimes produced houses of gargantuan proportions.

A big house, filled with family guests and servants, might be as populous as a small village. Servants, and particularly male servants, were engaged for reasons of social prestige as much as household management ... . When the establishment of Grimsthorpe was looked into following Lady Willoughby's death in 1828, there were ten male servants about the house and stables but a further sixteen on the estate and plantations, ten in the gardens, and ten looking after the park and the game preserves, making a grand total of forty-six.

The influence of the great house was most powerful in the village or villages immediately adjacent to it where a high proportion of the population was directly dependent on it for employment. ... . the influence of the great landowners was largely determined by the extent of their locally dispensed bounty and their charitable subscriptions

New Wealth

County society was difficult to penetrate, but it was not totally exclusive. The most important group was the bankers who did not have to struggle against the social disadvantage of having made their money in trade. Lawyers had much more trouble in unlocking social doors.

George Tennyson of Tealby, the grandfather of Alfred (Lord) Tennyson, was not only a very successful businessman and confidant of several Lindsey gentry, but also a substantial landowner in his own right. But his pretensions were not much relished by those who could recall his origins as a young lawyer in an attorney's office.

*In the last quarter of the century the fortunes on which to build dynasties were no longer being made in the Lincolnshire countryside. ... ... New wealth was now represented by urban businesses, the ironfounders, merchants and shipowners. ... ... In the late nineteenth century more fortunes were being made at Grimsby than anywhere else in the county, but it is remarkable how few Grimsby capitalists set themselves up as coutry gentlemen. In the early twentieth century the **Wintringhams** settled at Little Grimsby and branches of the Bennett family at Brackenborough and Oxcombe. But the Doughtys, Bannisters, Smethursts and Sutcliffes appear to have contented themselves with more suburban grandeur.*

The Middling Sort *(Chapter III)*
"And so we watch the new aristocracy leavening the old."
John Betjeman, 'Middle Class Architecture'.[6]

Attorneys, agents and bankers

The attorneys seldom made large fortunes, but they had unique opportunities for acquiring local influence. They touched the life of the rural community at more points than did the bankers and for the high-fliers the way to positions of trust and influence in the county was to attract the attention and patronage of the gentry and nobility. ... ... The sphere of most country solicitors, however, was the market town where they could build up extensive practices among the farmers and landowners. ... ... Banking in nineteenth century Lincolnshire was closely connected with the farming economy. The bankers were a small and highly respectable social group and banking (unlike trade) was still considered an acceptable occupation for gentlemen's sons.

Doctors and clergymen

Unlike the agents and attorneys, the doctors and clergymen stood at one remove from the rural economy. They aimed to acquire the confidence of all classes and their primary objective was not to make money but to minister to the needs of their neighbours. The squire and the labourer were alike prone to sickness and to sin and doctors and parsons aimed to acquire the confidence of all classes.. ... Nevertheless neither clergy nor medical men could stand outside the class system of rural society. Their status was defined partly by their income and family background, and partly by their education and professional training.

*The clergy, with their university degrees and distinctive dress, approached most nearly to a social caste, but there were wide variations within the clerical body. At the head of the country clergy were the relatives of the aristocracy, men like the Rev. Edward Chaplin of Blankney or the Rev F.C. **Massingberd** of South Ormsby* (and Rev. W.A. **Purey-Cust** of Belton and the **Thorolds** of Marston), *all holders of good family livings ... Some beneficed clergymen enjoyed the income of lesser squires. ... ... Massingberd, indeed, achieved wider distinction. As a comparatively young man he wrote a highly regarded book on the Reformation and later, in 1862, became chancellor of Lincoln cathedral. The social position* *of clergymen was also sometimes dictated by local factors beyond their control. Often, where a large landowner was non-resident, a parson would stand in as his representative in the district.*

Farming families and fortunes

The farmers of Lincolnshire varied so widely in wealth and style of living that it is almost meaningless to describe them as middle class. .... The wold farmers of the mid nineteenth century were not gentry, although they sometimes received the appellation of 'squire' from their neighbours. They were sometimes of good grammar school education and some even sent their sons to university. They lived in large houses that had in some cases been manor houses, with three or four indoor servants. They would keep a chaise or gig, riding horses, and probably hunters as well. Their wives, though they would attend to household chores in the morning, would pay and receive afternoon calls in a ladylike manner, their refinement no doubt contrasting in some cases with the market-place manners of their husbands.

Farmers, unlike the gentry, did not believe in primogeniture (inheritance by the eldest son)*. When they died they liked to leave their property equally between their sons. ... ... After the middle of the century there were more opportunities for losing than for making fortunes, and by 1900 many of the wold farming dynasties were extinct.*

Old style and new style farmers

The old style farmer had no doubt made money by his efforts, but his success had not given him ideas above his station. He thought in terms of a local community in which he had a recognised place. ... ... It is impossible to say that at a certain point the new style farmer ousted the old style farmer. It was rather a matter of the penetration of successive layers of farming society by social and economic ideas that were themselves changing and developing. Farmers may have shown less 'gratitude' to their landlords in times of depression, but at other times even those farmers who 'layed field to field' still tended to defer to the gentry in political and other matters.

A view of changes in the attitudes and behaviour of farmers is expressed in the following lines, quoted by Jabez Good of Burgh-le-Marsh

Agricultural Customs in 1800
Farmers at the plough.
Wife milking cow.
Daughter spinning yarn.
Son thrashing in the barn.
All happy to a charm.

Agricultural Customs 1900
Father gone to see the show.
Daughter at the pian-o.
Madame gaily dressed in satin.
All the boys learning Latin.
With a mortgage on the farm.

Commerce and crafts

Craftsmen ranged from solitary workers to owners of substantial businesses. The tradesman, that is the retailer, was an urban phenomenon that spread to the countryside as items such as tea and sugar spread to the rural diet.

By 1856 even the smallest village had a shopkeeper and in a moderate sized Lincolnshire village, the leading craftsmen and tradesmen, together with the innkeeper and carriers, probably influenced local opinion more than the clergymen, who belonged to a different class, or the larger farmers, who often lived outside the main settlement.

In nineteenth century Lincolnshire, business failures were common. Farmers drank themselves to death and suicides were frequent in bad times. Perhaps towards the end of the century life became more secure, but the opportunities for making fortunes had certainly diminished.

Farm labour and village life (Chapter IV)
Conflicting cultures

The Church had taken the lead in establishing day schools in the county, and it had clung to that lead with great tenacity throughout the nineteenth century, despite the strength of nonconformity in Lincolnshire. ... The education provided by the National schools in the smaller villages was certainly not favourable to the old culture. It was supervised by parsons whose own cultural background was an alien one. ... ... The curriculum was narrow and tedious and subjects were rarely related to the immediate experience of the pupils. For the brighter boys the chance to acquire a neat hand and some proficiency with figures may well have spoiled them for farm work ....

The early Methodists set their faces determinedly against many aspects of the old culture. .... Though not energetic providers of day schools the Methodists gave a great stimulus to adult education through their bible readings and class meetings. Methodism grew best where the forces of the Establishment were weakest and the open villages became its strongholds. ... ... Methodism struck at two centres of the old parish community, the church and the public house. ... ... In the wake of the Methodists, with their new standards of respectability, came the Temperance reformers.

The old culture was slow to die for it was not lacking in the strength and suppleness to adapt itself to changing conditions. It was defeated in the end, but as much by the depression in agriculture and the exodus from the countryside as by the assaults of urban culture.

The County in 1900   (Chapter IX)

More than many counties, Lincolnshire in 1900 was visually and architecturally a product of the preceding hundred years. New farmhouses were built for the new-style farmers, and new sheds and yards for their improved livestock. Cottages were run up for the rapidly growing rural population, and village brickyards multiplied to keep up with the rapidly growing demand.

Many churches in the county had been restored or completely rebuilt in the middle years of the century. The money came partly from wealthy benefactors, but large sums were raised by often small and poor congregations. By 1850, most villages had a neat low school-room and a small box-like Methodist chapel. After the middle of the century, chapels grew in size as building mania and architectural pretension seized village societies. In some places it was the chapel, not the church, that became the dominant architectural feature of the village.

All these changes affected the regional balance which gradually shifted from the south towards the north. In the early 1800's much of the county's activity and prosperity had been concentrated in the southern gentrified uplands of Kesteven and the wolds of south-eastern Lindsey. By the late 1800's all the most rapidly improving areas were in the north and west of the county and by 1900 the nobility and gentry no longer dominated county affairs. The legacy of Georgian Lincolnshire had come to an end.

These echoes of the nineteenth century may still be heard in Betjeman's glorious Lincolnshire. The county is, as yet, relatively unhampered by motorways and the convenience of high speed trains. At the beginning of the twenty-first century, byways of nostalgia are still with us. Perhaps we are, after all, not yet out of the 'transition period' between the old order and the new. But, for how long?

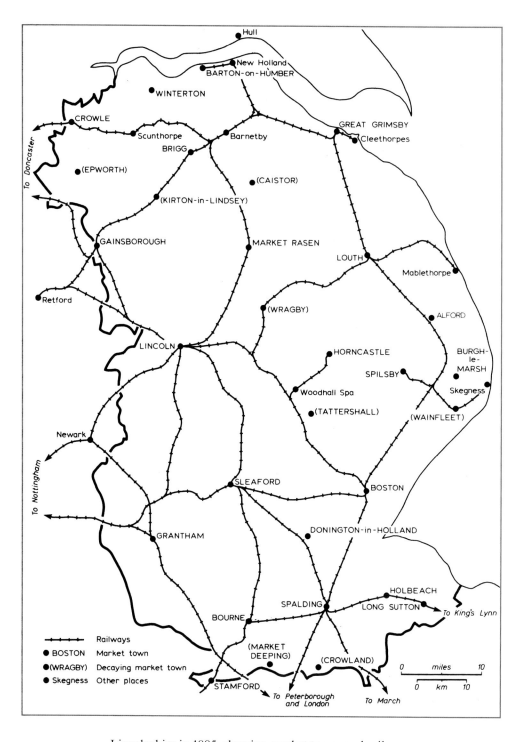

Lincolnshire in 1885, showing market towns and railways

Pre-Beeching
a Lincolnshire experience

by Jill Rundle

I once had a dream that I rode on a train
From Mareham-le-Fen up to Kirkby-on-Bain
Then Tumby and Coningsby, not very far,
To Tattershall, Kirkstead and then Woodhall Spa.
As Martin and Timberland slowly went by
The train chuffed contentedly, happy was I.

But, all of a sudden, it gathered up steam
And seemed to go mad as it ruined my dream.
From Braceby and Laceby to Wood Enderby,
Then Humby and Mumby and Sutton on Sea.
From Aby to Swaby and straight up to Louth,
Next Old Leake and New Leake and Kime (North and South).
And so the train rushed through the Lincolnshire names,
Goodbye Market Deeping and Deeping St James.
Hello Potterhanworth and Thornton le Moor
And Tattershall Thorpe – have we been here before?
Oh look, there's Old Bolingbroke, can we alight?
No, Holton-cum-Beckering's there on the right.
Grimsthorpe and Cowbit and Gedney Drove End,
The train lurched past Markby and stalled on a bend.
And I tumbled out as the train steamed and hissed,
And with a faint sigh just dissolved in the mist.

Railway Spirits

by Jill Rundle

To the ghostly Alford station
Run the never ending trains
Steam erupting from the engines,
Condensation on the panes.

Coming now from Louth and Grimsby,
Locally from Willoughby;
This one's heading off to London
What a splendid sight to see.

Passengers arrive to board here,
Old and young, their spirits come.
Milk train, school train, one for shoppers,
Sister, brother, Dad and Mum.

What a bustle, what a hurry,
As the spectres all appear,
Guard and porter, ticket seller,
Look, the station master's here.

But, alas, the scene is soundless,
Ghostly folk have silent tread,
Alford Station lies in history,
We have Beechings Way instead.

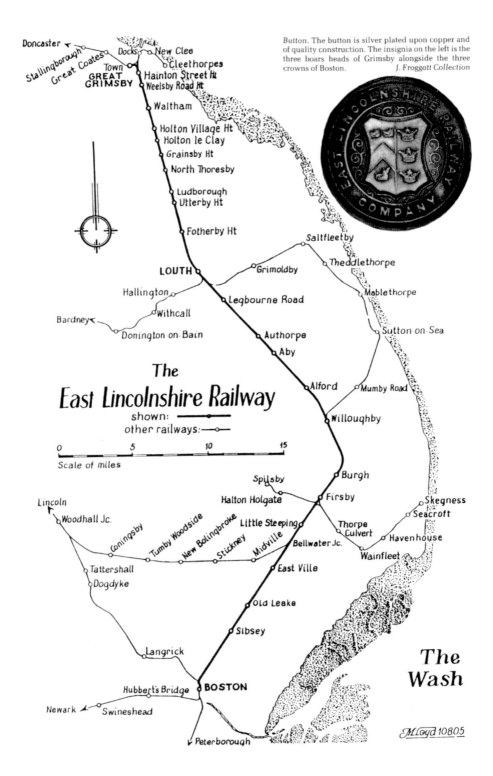

Button. The button is silver plated upon copper and of quality construction. The insignia on the left is the three boars heads of Grimsby alongside the three crowns of Boston. *J. Froggatt Collection*

The
East Lincolnshire Railway
shown: ●————●
other railways:—○—

0   5   10   15

Scale of miles

The Wash

The East Lincolnshire Railway, opened in 1848, provided a direct link with London for Boston, Louth and Great Grimsby. It was closed as a through route in 1970.

Bradshaw Redivivus….in Lincolnshire

by John Langford

It is hardly a secret that John Betjeman loved railways, whether the obscure gas-lit suburban stations in the environs of big cities, or the forgotten rural lines that in his day meandered across the length and breadth of England.

Lincolnshire would have presented a happy hunting ground for the sort of railway ramblings that Betjeman enjoyed and it is pleasurable to think of his travelling in some ancient wooden-bodied Great Northern carriage from Bardney to Louth, or from Firsby to Spilsby, or from Woodhall Junction to Horncastle. All these lines had infrequent passenger trains, perhaps five or six a day even in their heyday, and all succumbed to the onslaught of the road-motor long before the Beeching era of the mid-1960's. The Lincolnshire railway network as it was in 1885 is shown on page 118

Published references to John Betjeman's railway journeys in Lincolnshire are not numerous, but one line that he probably used was the 'East Lincolnshire Railway'. It was opened in 1848 and provided a direct link with London for the following 122 years.

If travelling from London, Betjeman would almost certainly have used the line on more than one occasion to visit his friend Jack Yates in Louth. The route from Boston to Grimsby is shown on page 122. He might well have caught the Grimsby express from Kings Cross, taking luncheon or afternoon tea in the dining car perhaps. The train turned off today's GNER main line at Werrington Junction, north of Peterborough, to serve Spalding, Boston, Firsby (for Skegness), Louth and Grimsby. He would have seen that Boston had a good station and a signal-box called Maud Foster, near where the railway crossed diagonally over the River Witham.

John Betjeman addressed the local Naturalist and Literary Society at Louth Town Hall on the evening of Wednesday 4th November 1953, his subject *'Louth and Victorian Architecture'*. The lecture was in fact on behalf of the recently formed LOCT, the Lincolnshire Old Churches Trust. Referring to Betjeman's journey, the (Louth) Advertiser for Saturday 7th November reported:

'Lincolnshire appealed to him because of the extent of its skyline which was so vast. He referred to his journey to Louth from Peterborough on a slow train and saw evidence of that every time he looked at it. In particular he mentioned Aby station, which was beautifully kept with well-kept hedges and flowers which were still in bloom now.

Mr Betjeman went on to pay a tribute to the architecture of Louth station which was built just over 100 years ago.'

The Peterborough to Grimsby main line through East Lincolnshire was closed as a through route in 1970, though the sections as far as Spalding and from Boston to (just short of) Firsby are still open. They now form parts of cross-country routes from Peterborough to Lincoln and Nottingham to Skegness respectively.

Aby station, on the East Lincolnshire line between Alford and Louth in 1963.

Jack Yates, a bookseller of Louth, was of course one of the compilers of the *Shell Guide to Lincolnshire, (1965),* the other being Henry Thorold of Marston Hall near Grantham. The nearest stations to Marston Hall were Barkston, on the main line four miles north of Grantham, and Hougham, another two miles beyond. It is enticing to think of Henry Thorold being driven to one of these remote stations to collect J.B. off the train. But they both had pitifully sparse services, even in J.B.'s day, and it is likely that he had to be content with the longer road journey of some five and a half miles from Grantham. Barkston station closed to passenger traffic in 1955 and Hougham in 1957.

Alford town station was closed in 1970. The road to it is now named Beechings Way.

It would be nice to think of John Betjeman and John Piper carrying out some of their church-crawling to remote Lincolnshire churches, travelling by branch line train and perhaps by local bus. But with the services as they were and the remoteness of some of the villages - even from the stations that purported to serve them - this must remain a pipe-dream among the many railway aficionados who also devote their time to following in Betjeman's footsteps, either actually or spiritually, with *Bradshaw's Guide* at their right hand.

But Betjeman would have appreciated much of the early railway architecture of Lincolnshire, several remnants of which are still with us, even if some of the stations concerned have not seen any passenger trains for many years. The main station building at Louth, already mentioned, would be an example:

> *'solidly built like an Elizabethan manor-house, but .... sadly dwarfed by the concrete maltings, an epitaph in brick and stone to the decline of the railways'*.[1]

A print of the elegant and impressive Louth railway station in 1848

The lovely Italianate creations on the Lincoln to Boston line, of which Woodhall Junction (now a private residence) and Tattershall (now a pottery) are still nice examples, lost their trains in 1970 or earlier.

It would be good to think that John Betjeman experienced Lincolnshire's bracing seaside at Skegness by using the railway from Nottingham, through Grantham, Sleaford and Boston (this remains with us, of course). Or perhaps he tried Sutton-on-Sea or Mablethorpe, by changing off a Grimsby train at Willoughby, another remote country junction of the sort Betjeman loved.

In the absence of documentary evidence, much of the foregoing is mild conjecture but we do know that Betjeman and Jack Yates enjoyed sorties from Louth, though I doubt if they ever took the grand picnic hamper with them when they travelled on the local country buses which 'carried besides the passengers, chickens, ducklings, piglets and sacks of produce'.[2] If they did go, as is suggested, to Brocklesby Park, seat of the Earls of Yarborough, I hope they called at Brocklesby railway station (only closed in recent years), 'a lively Jacobean composition with early Dutch gables', to quote one commentator.

Another long cross-country line that Betjeman must have used at some stage was the Midland and Great Northern Joint Railway, which stretched from Little Bytham (end-on junction with the Midland Railway from Leicester and beyond) through Bourne, Spalding, Sutton Bridge, South Lynn and Melton Constable (the railway's locomotive headquarters in the early days) to the Norfolk coast at Sheringham, Cromer and Great Yarmouth. Another branch led to Norwich City.

Bourne would have interested Betjeman as the station house, in local hand-made brick, was formerly Red Hall – a comparatively rare example of the railway taking over a much older building for their use. Another example was Staines West, GWR, previously a mustard miller's house. After closure of the M & GN, Bourne station reverted to civilian use becoming local council property. WEA day courses – one on John Betjeman recently – take place in the rooms of the building.

Red Hall, Bourne.
Purchased by Bourne and Essendine Railway in the late 1850's and used as a station house from its opening until final closure of M & GN in 1959

Both of the railway stations in the town of Stamford, admired so much by Betjeman, are architectural pieces in local stone of good date. The Midland station, by Sancton Wood, 1848 (still active of course) is in a Tudor style without being too ornate and sports S & PR – Syston and Peterborough Railway – on the weathervane of the tower. The little two-platformed terminus called Stamford East – Stamford and Essendine Railway 1856, closed in 1957 – has a splendid symmetrical frontage with a strong Elizabethan flavour. It is happily still well cared for as residential accommodation.

Stamford East – ER/GNR
The station frontage (1856) is now in residential use.

John Betjeman loved double-barrelled station names and several (outside Lincolnshire) appear in his writings, sometimes mildly disguised: 'Woodford & Hinton' and 'Braintree & Bocking' come to mind. How he would have warmed to three consecutive stations on the Lincoln to Sleaford line : 'Nocton & Dunston', 'Blankney & Metheringham', and 'Scopwick & Timberland'! Or south of Sleaford: 'Aswarby & Scredington' and 'Billingborough & Horbling'.

As far as appears to be recorded, John Betjeman was 'first excited by the county', when he visited his friend Noel Blakiston at Kirkby-on-Bain in the 1920's, a nice journey for any ferroviaphile. Kirkby-on-Bain is a village some four and a half miles south of Horncastle, the nearest railway stations being Woodhall Spa - 'that unexpected Bournemouth-like settlement in the middle of Lincolnshire'[3] – or Coningsby, on the little line that used to go across the Fens from Woodhall Junction to Bellwater Junction (no station here, just a lonely signal box) south west of Firsby. So one can conjure up the good Canon Felix Blakiston and his son collecting a much younger John Betjeman in the 1920's from one of these places, or perhaps from Woodhall Junction or Tattershall on the through Lincoln to Boston line.

And we haven't even mentioned Lincoln station itself, or Lincoln Central as it was of course. Happily it remains largely intact with its through-roads for goods traffic, footbridges and busy level-crossings - and that first view of Lincoln Cathedral seen from the train east or west of the city. I don't think anyone can take that away from us!

John Betjeman's favourite station in Lincolnshire? We have come across some evidence that it was Harmston, just south of Lincoln on the Grantham line. Perhaps he would have liked to have been appointed station master there. (He said this of Blake Hall station on the Ongar line, allegedly the least used London Transport station).

So Betjeman loved his Lincolnshire and may have travelled quite extensively over the one-time main lines through the county, and on those many delightful branches that then connected even the smallest towns and villages with the outside world. Further research through letters and documents may yet bring to light details of such travels.

The Purey-Cust family in Lincolnshire

by Kit Lawie

'You hold yourself erect and every step
Bounced up and down as though you walked on springs.
Your ice-blue eyes, your lashes long and light,
Your sweetly freckled face and turned up nose
So haunted me that all my loves since then
Have had a look of Peggy Purey-Cust.'

'Summoned by Bells'[1]

Peggy Purey-Cust, Betjeman's first love, was related to a distinguished and titled Lincolnshire family. She was the great-great-grand-daughter of an earl, grand-daughter of the Dean of York and daughter of an Admiral. Another of her family, a great-uncle, was successively headmaster of Harrow, Bishop of Ripon and Durham and Archbishop of Canterbury. Yet another ancestor, an early Cust, was Speaker of the House of Commons from 1761-70.

Belton, near Grantham in Lincolnshire was the home of the Brownlow and Cust families and, although now owned by the National Trust, it still echoes life as it once was in the perfect English country house.

The Orangery at Belton House

129

Peggy's uncle, the Reverend William Purey-Cust, was made rector of Belton in 1882. He held the living at Belton for nearly 30 years from 1882 to 1910 and it was at the rectory of Belton that his daughters Alice, Mary, Gwen, Norah and son, Richard, were born.

It was there that my mother, born and brought up near Belton, first met his daughters. One of her early memories was being taken by Alice, who was then in her early teens and six years older than mother, to see the Orangery at Belton House where her relative Lord Brownlow lived. As a teenager my mother knew the rector's daughters until they moved with their father from Belton to the Lincoln rectory of St Peter's, Eastgate in 1910. Less than ten years later their mother died in Lincoln, during the flu epidemic at the end of the 1914-18 war.

The rector's son, Richard, joined the Royal Artillery and became a very distinguished soldier. He was awarded a C.B.E. D.S.O. and M.C. and was made a Brigadier. He died in 1958 aged 69.

Memorial to Richard Brownlow Purey-Cust in Belton church

In the meantime, Mother had come to live at East Keal and, by 1925, the Rev. Canon Purey-Cust, as he now was, had taken the living at nearby Skendleby from where in 1935 he retired to West Keal Hall. It was while at Skendleby that Alice and Mary worked on a labour of love, lasting many years, to produce a large wool carpet that reached from the chancel steps to the altar. This colourfully rich carpet is still in place after 70 years.

And so from nearby West Keal it was that Alice sought my mother on hearing she lived within walking distance. Her visits were a breath of fresh air. By then in her 50's she would come puffing up to our farmstead after climbing Marden Hill, her Sealyham's leash looped over her arm. The state of the weather seemed to have no effect on her, rain, hail or snow. One Christmas Eve found her on our doorstep having trudged through a storm to bring gifts for my ten year old brother and me. So kind and friendly and a little eccentric. She was not unlike the actress Margaret Rutherford as Madame Arcarti in 'Blythe Spirit'.

She walked through the lanes of Mavis Enderby and Old Bolingbroke nearly always reading from a book held before her face. Could it have been an early publication of 'Continual Dew'? I think mother would have known! They shared an interest in J.B.'s work from the late 1930's onwards and quoted verses from him. They discussed poetry and the current troubles with Oswald Moseley and strangely I remember the name Hore Belisha (Secretary of State at that time). As children my brother and I found this name fascinating and took to using it as a mild expletive when out of earshot of parents.

By December 1936 they were talking about the abdication crisis (the news by then was in the press). It must have interested the Purey-Custs greatly since their cousin Peregrine (Lord Brownlow) was friend and Lord in Waiting to Edward VIII. through the accession and through his affair with Wallis Simpson. He'd offered Belton House to the King as a haven as he dealt with his contacts with the press and Prime Minister Baldwin.

Lord Brownlow in 1970

was Lord in Waiting to Edward VIII
and Lord Lieutenant of Lincolnshire,
1936-50

As the unmarried daughters of gentry the Purey-Cust sisters had never done paid work but through the war they did voluntary work of various kinds. Mary was the County Commissioner of the Girl Guides in the 30's and, as a tenderfoot in the Keal company, I held her in great awe. She was very tall and distinguished-looking in her gold braided uniform, more serious in manner than Alice and very like her father in looks. The Rev. Purey-Cust was in his 80's when I met him, a man of great stature and dignity when, as school-children, we sang carols at West Keal Hall on Christmas morning.

Miss Mary Purey-Cust, second from the left, with members of the Spilsby detachment of the Red Cross in the early years of the war.

Not long after his death in late 1939 Alice and Mary moved to a much smaller house in Spilsby where they spent most of the 1939-45 war years without staff. They named the house, appropriately, 'Belton'. When given a rabbit by a neighbour, to eke out the rations, they had no idea how to cook it and so it went straight into their oven complete with skin and head! The result, one hopes, was then buried in the garden. As they became more elderly they moved to a little bungalow in Raithby Road, Hundleby. By 1962 they had both died.

This branch of the Purey-Custs was a highly respected family with regard for duty and kindness but they appeared to be not at all well off. It was through knowing them that I came to know of John Betjeman and his poetry - not as most people probably first knew of the poet before hearing of the name Peggy Purey-Cust. In the words of the Rev. Robert LLoyd, whose father was Peggy's cousin: "If she had been called Peggy Smith would she have been enshrined in *Summoned by Bells?"* As he said "It is a useless question." But the converse was nevertheless voiced at a recent meeting when it was suggested that J.B. had probably made up the name 'Peggy Purey-Cust' because it sounded noble and aristocratic! The idea, of course, would be met with scorn by Betjeman Society members, not least by me.

To perpetuate the Lincolnshire connection, Alice's brother Richard Brownlow Purey-Cust and his wife named their cottage in Dorset "Pinchbeck".

The Purey-Cust family tree

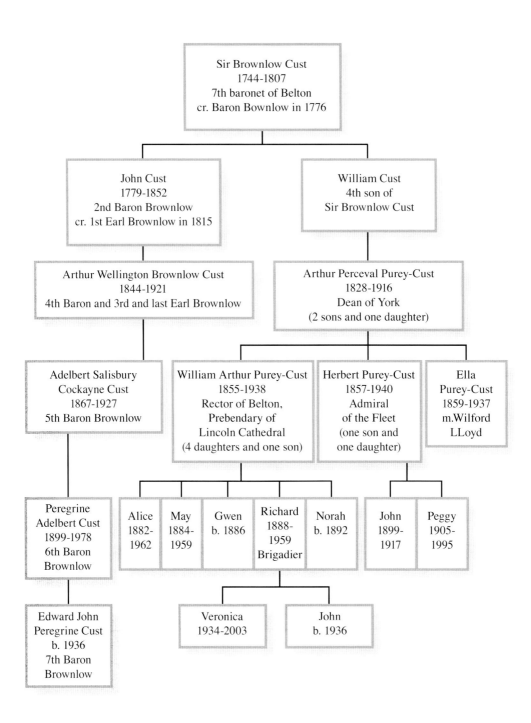

Sir Brownlow Cust
1744-1807
7th baronet of Belton
cr. Baron Bownlow in 1776

John Cust
1779-1852
2nd Baron Brownlow
cr. 1st Earl Brownlow in 1815

William Cust
4th son of
Sir Brownlow Cust

Arthur Wellington Brownlow Cust
1844-1921
4th Baron and 3rd and last Earl Brownlow

Arthur Perceval Purey-Cust
1828-1916
Dean of York
(2 sons and one daughter)

Adelbert Salisbury
Cockayne Cust
1867-1927
5th Baron Brownlow

William Arthur Purey-Cust
1855-1938
Rector of Belton,
Prebendary of
Lincoln Cathedral
(4 daughters and one son)

Herbert Purey-Cust
1857-1940
Admiral
of the Fleet
(one son and
one daughter)

Ella
Purey-Cust
1859-1937
m.Wilford
LLoyd

Peregrine
Adelbert Cust
1899-1978
6th Baron
Brownlow

Alice
1882-
1962

May
1884-
1959

Gwen
b. 1886

Richard
1888-
1959
Brigadier

Norah
b. 1892

John
1899-
1917

Peggy
1905-
1995

Edward John
Peregrine Cust
b. 1936
7th Baron
Brownlow

Veronica
1934-2003

John
b. 1936

Pedigree of a first love

by Michael Richardson

'At the top of the hill lived John's 'first and purest love'. .... 'Satchel on back, he used to hurry up West Hill to catch her as she walked to school accompanied by her nanny' [1]

Peggy Purey-Cust lived in London in a large Georgian house at the top of a steep hill from Gospel Oak to Highgate village. John Betjeman lived on the lower, more modest, slopes of the same road in a semi-detached house.

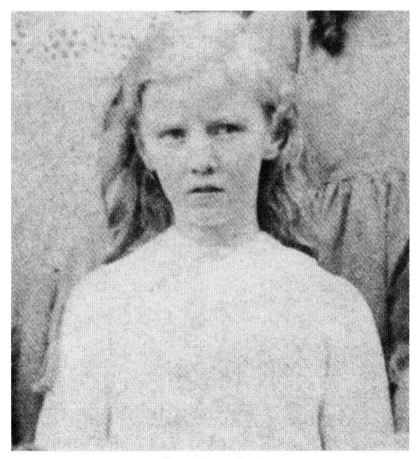

Peggy Purey-Cust

Peggy was the daughter of an Admiral of the Fleet. Her pedigree was impeccable and in marked contrast to that of Betjeman's parents. There was, however, a link between them that would have intrigued him if he had known of it as they walked to school in Highgate. The village of Pinchbeck in Lincolnshire, had been the family home of Betjeman's mother, Mabel Bessie Dawson. It was also the home of Peggy's early ancestors, the Custs who, in the sixteenth century, had been lords of the manor of Pinchbeck. The family tree on page 134 shows the Lincolnshire links of the Brownlow, Cust and Purey-Cust families..

Peggy's grandfather, **Arthur Perceval Purey-Cust (1828-1916)** was the first of the Custs to put Purey before the family name. He was the son of the Hon. William Cust and a grandson of Sir Brownlow Cust.

Born in 1828, he was educated at the Proprietary School, Lee, in Kent and Brasenose College, Oxford. He was a Fellow of All Souls College from 1850-54 and he was ordained in 1851. He married Lady Emma Bess Bligh, daughter of the 5th Earl of Darnley in 1854.

Following his ordination A. P. Purey-Cust was:

> Rector of Cheddington, Bucks and Rural Dean 1853-62,
> Vicar of St Mary's Reading and Rural Dean 1862-75
> Vicar of Aylesbury 1875-76
> Archdeacon of Buckingham 1875-80
> Chaplain to the Archbishop of Canterbury 1868; and
> Dean of York 1880-1916

When his much-loved predecessor at York, Dean Duncombe, died on 6th January 1880 there was a strong desire in the city to have a successor as like him as possible.

Purey-Cust, like Duncombe, was of a noble family, married into a noble family, a man with private means and a strong but moderate high churchman. He accepted the Deanery of York on 18th February 1880.

More artistic than Duncombe, he was a little more absent-minded, In a letter about drains he once spelt the Deanery the Drainery. But, though he was not a Duncombe, he was excellent as a continuer of Duncombe's work:

> *always in the Minster, never away, caring about every stone and every service, generous with his money and his affections, much liked and often revered in the city, artistic, an antiquarian by taste who wrote on the Minster heraldry and of its history and monuments'* [2]

During his time as dean, the west window had its glass and mullions repaired, the glass of the chapter house and the five sisters window was preserved, and the parapet of the central tower was restored. But the restoration of the entire west front (1907) was the supreme achievement of Purey-Cust's time in York and the fondly remembered benevolent paternalism of Duncombe towards the workmen was extended by his successor with substantial tea-parties to celebrate the end of a repair as well as more modest domestic events.

The long reign of Purey-Cust was a quiet and steady time. But by 1914 he was old and decrepit. In 1916 zeppelins floated across York, dropping a bomb within a few hundred yards of the Minster. Archbishop Lang went to the dean and insisted that the glass be removed from the Minster windows and buried for safety. With tears running down his face the dean pleaded that he was too old to oversee such a work; and it led to his death. He caught a fatal chill while surveying the windows and he died at Christmas 1916 at the age of 88.

Arthur Perceval Purey-Cust, Dean of York

Dean Purey-Cust had three children, all born in the early years after his marriage while he was rector of his first parish in Buckinghamshire.

William Arthur Purey-Cust (1855-1938) was Peggy Purey-Cust's 'Uncle Willie'. He was the elder son of the dean of York and a graduate of Christ Church, Oxford. Like his father he read theology and he was the only one of the Purey-Custs to spend all of his adult life in Lincolnshire. His first parish was at Belton, where the seventeenth century Belton House was the country seat of his uncle, the 5th Baron Brownlow.

Peggy's Uncle Willie was:

Vicar of Belton	1882-1910
of St Peter, Eastgate, Lincoln	1910-25
of St Peter and St Paul, Skendleby	1925-35

and he was a canon and prebendary of Farendon in Lincoln cathedral.

He had four daughters and a son. All of them were born during his time at Belton. But like so many girls who were growing up during the first war, only one of his daughters got married.

After their mother died in 1918, the two eldest of his daughters, **Alice** and **Mary**, lived with and looked after him for the rest of his life. He retired from the living at Skendleby at the age of 80 and then moved to West Keal Hall near Spilsby, where he lived for the last three years of his life.

His third daughter **Gwen** married a brigadier in 1932. After he died a few years later, she lived in Ham, near Kew, with her youngest sister **Norah.**

Canon Purey Cust's son **Richard** was a distinguished soldier. He joined the Royal Artillery, became a Brigadier, and was awarded a D.S.O. and M.C. Richard Purey-Cust had two children:

- a daughter, **Veronica**, who married a Swiss and lived in Vancouver. She died in 1993, and
- a son, **John** (b. 1936), who is still alive. He lives in New Zealand and was a forestry adviser to the New Zealand government. He never married and is now the only surviving Purey-Cust.

Herbert Purey-Cust (1857-1940)

was Peggy PC's father. He became Admiral Sir Herbert PC. and he lived in a large Georgian house at the top of West Hill, Highgate.

He had two children. His son **John** was killed at the Battle of Jutland, a midshipman aged 17. His daughter **Peggy** was Betjeman's childhood sweetheart. But, like many other young girls born at the turn of the century, she never married.

The admiral's family evacuated to Minehead in 1939 and Peggy's parents both died there during the war. All their furniture from Highgate, left in store in London, was destroyed in an air raid.

Apart from six or seven years in Australia, where she went to care for an elderly relative of her mother's, Peggy lived in Minehead until she was over 90. She died there in 1995.

Ella Purey-Cust (1859-1937)

married Wilford LLoyd C.B. C.V.O. (1855-1935). They had two children: **Humphrey** (1893-1966) who was Gentleman Usher to the Queen, and **Victoria** (1897-1980) who never married.

Humphrey's son **Robert** (b.1918) and his younger cousin from New Zealand (John) are the only surviving descendants of their great-grandfather, the Dean of York. In 1988 Robert LLoyd became the first chairman of the Canterbury Branch of the Betjeman Society.

Tribute to J.B.

By Jill Rundle

Sir John, could you guess when you lived on West Hill,
And walked on the Heath where you wandered at will,
And tried to write poems, aged seven or eight,
That many years later your fame would be great?
With sun on St. Michael's and shouts from the Ponds,
With sheep on the slopes, and the elm trees beyond,
You sought inspiration, for better, for worse,
You knew from a boy that you had to write verse.
And as a shy child, full of longings and fears,
With Archibald bear bringing comfort to tears,
And hot buttered toast and a ride in a train,
And beautiful Peggy to love, though in vain –

In all this lost time of your cosy clad youth,
Could you have imagined the present vast truth?
A century later your work is alive.
The J.B. society continues to thrive.
Our late Poet Laureate your verses live on,
And people remember you kindly, Sir John.

Illustrations

Maps and Diagrams

Acknowledgements

With thanks to all contributors to this book. Our particular appreciation is due to the following for permission to use material identified in the lists of illustrations, maps and diagrams. Members of the Betjeman Society are indicated thus (XX*)

(SC*)	Stuart Crooks
(CK*)	Clifford Knowles
(CJ/VWF)	Cressida Jupp/Virginia Wintringham Flew
(HLC)	History of Lincolnshire Committee
(HCS)	Horncastle Civic Society
(HYM)	'History of York Minster', Clarendon Press, Oxford 1977
(JMM)	John Montgomery Massingberd
(JK*)	John Ketteringham
(JL*)	John Langford
(KL*)	Kit Lawie
(HL*)	Horace Liberty
(LCC)	Lincolnshire County Council
(LL)	Lincolnshire Life
(RL*)	Rodney Lines
(WM)	Miss Winifred Macdonald
(NT)	National Trust
(OP)	Oakwood Press
(MR*)	Michael Richardson
(MS)	Mrs Maisie Sewards
(SPS)	Skegness Publicity Services
(MT*)	Michael Thomas

We have made every effort to identify copyright holders and to obtain their permission, but would be glad to hear of any inadvertent errors or omissions.

Contributors

*Stuart E Crooks Director of the Lincolnshire Wildlife Trust for over twenty years. Has a special interest in the interactions between landscape, ecology, people and the county's literary connections.

Cressida Jupp & Virginia Wintringham Flew Daughters of Edmund Penning-Rowsell and Margaret Wintringham.

*John Ketteringham, MBE. Lincolnshire born author of books on Lincolnshire people and local history. His magnum opus is 'Lincolnshire Bells and Bell-founders'.

*Clifford Knowles Retired vicar. Fellow of the Royal Photographic Society with a passionate interest in church architecture and fine art photography.

*John Langford Aficionado of John Betjeman, our landscape, our railways, and many of the other good things in life.

*Kit Lawie Locally born with farming background. Writes short stories and researches and writes on local history.

*Horace Liberty Retired schoolteacher and associate lecturer with the Open University. Avid collector of betjemania and regular contributor to the journal of the Betjeman Society.

*Rodney Lines Former WEA tutor-organiser in Lincolnshire, poetry lecturer. Vice-President of the John Clare Society and Chairman of the Robert Bloomfield Society.

*Michael Richardson Retired planner with life-long interest in people and places.

David Robinson, OBE. President of Louth Naturalists, Antiquarian & Literary Society. Retired University of Nottingham resident tutor, Former editor of 'Lincolnshire Life'.

*Jill Rundle Retired teacher, interested in talking, literature and in writing murder mystery plays and poems, including one on the back of a menu card at the Ritz.

*Elizabeth Thomas A Yorkshire woman interested in dialect speech, history and music. Also a Janeite.

*Michael Thomas Main interests are in music, poetry and bell-ringing. Chairman of the Lincolnshire Branch of The Betjeman Society.

Jack Yates Co-author of the Shell Guide to Lincolnshire. Vice-Chairman of the Lincolnshire branch of the Council for the Preservation of Rural England and founder of Louth Civic Society. Died in 1971.

Notes and references

Where reference is given to *John Betjeman's Collected Poems*, this is the 'New Edition including Uncollected Poems', John Murray, London 2001

"Ah Lincolnshire, a lovely county"

(1)   Lincolnshire Echo (June/July 1972)
(2)   Louth Advertiser (7th November 1953)
(3)   George Crabbe, East Anglian poet (1754-1832)
(4)   Charles Dickens, *Bleak House* (Chapter 2)
(5)   Charles Kingsley, English author (1819-75)
(6)   Tennyson, *In Memoriam*
(7)   Tennyson, *The Idylls of the King*, The Last Tournament
(8)   BBC recording. *I Remember*. Diana (Lady) Montgomery-Massingberd interviewed by JB on 23rd June 1961, broadcast 30th June 1961
(9)   JB speech at the *Lincolnshire Past Present and Future Conference*, Theatre Royal, Lincoln, 2nd December 1963
(10)   Bevis Hillier, *John Betjeman: A Life in Pictures*, John Murray, London 1984, p28
(11)   (ed) Candida Lycett Green, *John Betjeman Letters Volume 2*, Methuen, London 1995, p347
(12)   Skegness Pier Orchestra Programme, 16th August 1908
(13)   Charles Tennyson Turner, *A Hundred Sonnets* selected with an introduction by JB   and Sir Charles Tennyson. Rupert Hart-Davis, London 1960
(14)   JB letter, 1968, to Precentor about chapel in Diocesan House, Wren Library collection, Lincoln Cathedral
(15)   (ed) Candida Lycett Green (1995), ibid, p303
(16)   (ed) Candida Lycett Green (1995), ibid, p572
(17)   letter from Peter Burton to Dr John Ketteringham
(18)   BBC recording. *I Remember*. Diana (Lady) Montgomery-Massingberd interviewed by JB on 23rd June 1961, broadcast 30th June 1961
(19)   Hugh Massingberd, letter of 10.06.2005 to M T
(20)   Grimsby Evening Telegraph, June/July 1961
(21)   A Lincolnshire Tale, *Collected Poems*, p91
(22)   House of Rest, *Collected Poems*, p161
(23)   JB letter to George Barnes, 18th June 1946, quoted by Bevis Hillier in *John Betjeman: New Fame, New Love*, John Murray, London 2002, p365
(24)   Jack Yates, *The Buildings of Louth*, Lincolnshire Life, Autumn 1962
(25)   (ed) Candida Lycett Green, *John Betjeman Letters Volume 1*, Methuen, London 1994, p65
(26)   Bevis Hillier, *Young Betjeman*, John Murray, London 1988, p291

Betjeman's Lincolnshire poetry and prose

(1)   A Lincolnshire Tale, *Collected Poems*, p91
(2)   House of Rest, *Collected Poems*, p161

(3)   John Betjeman *A Few Late Chrysanthemums*, John Murray, London 1954, p23
(4)   Death in Leamington, *Collected Poems*, p1
(5)   Felixstowe or The Last of Her Order, *Collected Poems*, p222
(6)   Sun and Fun, *Collected Poems*, p173
(7)   Remorse, *Collected Poems*, p182
(8)   A Lincolnshire Church, *Collected Poems*, p141
(9)   John Betjeman, *Ghastly Good Taste*, Anthony Blond Ltd, London 1970, p94
(10)   John Betjeman, *Lamp-posts and Landscape*, 'Light and Lighting', November 1953
(11)   John Betjeman, *Antiquarian Prejudice*, in *First and Last Loves*, John Murray, London 1952, p48-66
(12)   Ibid p54
(13)   Ibid p54
(14)   Ibid p55

House of Rest
(1)   John Betjeman, *Ghastly Good Taste,* Anthony Blond Ltd, London, 1970, p95
(2)   A Lincolnshire Tale, *Collected Poems*, p91
(3)   House of Rest, *Collected Poems,* p162

Lincoln
(1)   (ed) John Betjeman, *Collins Guide to English Parish Churches*, Collins, London   1958, p234
(2)   John Betjeman, *A Pictorial History of English Architecture*, John Murray, London   1972, p60
(3)   Ibid, p25
(4)   Ibid, p28
(5)   Ibid, p25
(6)   Ibid, p28
(7)   Ibid, p27
(8)   Ibid, p27
(9)   JB letter to Mr Harding, 11th October 1938, Lincolnshire Archives
(10)   Report on the *Lincolnshire Past Present and Future Conference*, Theatre Royal Lincoln, 2nd December 1963, in Lincolnshire Life, February 1964
(11)   Lincolnshire Chronicle, 6th December 1963
(12)   Lincolnshire Standard, 3rd December 1963
(13)   John Betjeman, *The English Town in the Last Hundred Years*, The Rede Lecture 1956, Cambridge University Press 1956, p24
(14)   JB letter to Iain Horobin, 15th November 1970, HL collection
(15)   John Betjeman, Foreword to Amery & Cruikshank, *The Rape of Britain*, Paul Elek, London 1975, p7
(16)   Frank Delaney, *Betjeman Country*, Hodder & Stoughton 1983, p13

Lincolnshire Landscapes

(1)   A Lincolnshire Tale, Cornhill Magazine, London, April 1945, later included in *Collected Poems*, p91

(2)   A Lincolnshire Church, *Collected Poems*, p141

(3)   Tennyson *In Memoriam*, Edward Moxon, London 1850

(4)   Tennyson, *The Brook*, an idyll in *Maud,* Edward Moxon, London 1855

(5)   BBC, Contrasts: *Tennyson – a Beginning and an End*, London, 17th December 1968

(6)   Thorold & Yates, Lincolnshire – A Shell Guide, Faber & Faber, London 1965, p12

(7)   A Lincolnshire Tale, op. cit.

Betjeman and Tennyson

(1)   BBC recording. *Alfred Lord Tennyson: Tennyson as Humourist.* Talk by JB with poems read by Sir Charles Tennyson, broadcast 3rd July 1950

(2)   Charles Tennyson Turner, *A Hundred Sonnets* (Selected with an introduction by Sir Charles Tennyson and JB), Rupert Hart-Davis, London 1960

(3)   BBC, Contrasts: *Tennyson – a Beginning and an End*, 17th December 1968

(4)   RB Martin, *Tennyson – The Unquiet Heart*, Faber & Faber, London 1980

(5)   Tregardock, *Collected Poems*, p239

(6)   (ed) Candida Lycett Green, *John Betjeman Letters Volume 2*, Methuen, London 1995, p416

(7)   Ibid p358

(8)   BBC broadcast, *Tennyson – Portrait of a Poet*, 24th July 1970

(9)   Ibid

(10)   RB Martin, op cit, p358

(11)   Middlesex, *Collected Poems*, p163

(12)   The Last Laugh, *Collected Poems*, p341

Lincolnshire Churches

(1)   (ed) John Betjeman, *Collins Guide to English Parish Churches*, Collins, London   1958, p234

(2)   Bevis Hillier, *John Betjeman: New Fame, New Love*, John Murray, London 2002, p365

(3)   John Betjeman, *Church Poems*, John Murray, London 1981, p8

(4)   Ibid p35

(5)   Bevis Hillier, *John Betjeman: New Fame, New Love*, John Murray, London 2002, p365

(6)   St Peter & Paul, Langton-by-Spilsby, Church Guide

(7)   St John the Baptist, Great Carlton, Church Guide

(8)   (ed) Nigel Kerr, *John Betjeman's Guide to English Parish Churches*, Harper Collins, London 1993, p353

(9)   (ed) John Betjeman, *Collins Guide to English Parish Churches*, Collins, London1958, p229

(10)   Ibid, p29

Theophilus Caleb at Huttoft

      Compiled with thanks to Kit Lawie and to John Timms for their assistance. Canons Michael Wright and John Swaby were also very helpful.

Jack Yates

(1)   Unpublished autobiography, location not now known

Betjeman at Sausthorpe

(1)   John Betjeman, *Summoned by Bells,* John Murray, London 1960

(2)   Carlos Sanchez was a local portrait painter. His Spanish father married Sheila Neal-Green of Holbeck Manor, Greetham, near Horncastle. He painted the portraits of the Kochans and the Italian mural at Sausthorpe in 1953.

(3)   Myfanwy, *Collected Poems*, p69

(4)   Myfanwy at Oxford, *Collected Poems*, p71

Life in Nineteenth Century Lincolnshire

(1)   John Betjeman *Ghastly Good Taste,* Anthony Blond Ltd., London 1970. pxxiii.

(2)   Ibid, p9-10

(3)   RJ Olney, *Rural Society and County Government in Nineteenth Century Lincolnshire,* History of Lincolnshire Committee, for the Society of Lincolnshire History and Archaeology, Lincoln 1979.

(4)   John Betjeman 1970, ibid, p95

(5)   Ibid, p1

(6)   Ibid, p92

Bradshaw Redivivus ... in Lincolnshire

      With thanks to Graham Hepper of Stephenson Way, Bourne, for contributing information on his one time local railway station and to Don Kennedy of Disraeli Road, Ealing, for some gems from *Britain's Historic Railway Buildings,* OUP 2003, by Gordon Biddle. The map on p112 and the illustrations of Louth, Aby and Alford stations on pps 114 and 115 are taken from *The East Lincolnshire Railway* by A.J. Ludlam (1991), and reproduced with the kind permission of Jane Kennedy, proprietor of the Oakwood Press, Usk, Monmouthshire.

(1)   Henry Thorold & Jack Yates, *Lincolnshire, a Shell Guide,* Faber & Faber, London 1965, p102

(2)   Bevis Hillier, *John Betjeman: New Fame, New Love,* John Murray, London 2002, p364

(3)   (ed) John Betjeman, *Collins Guide to English Parish Churches*, Collins, London 1958, p235

The Purey-Cust family in Lincolnshire

It is to the Rev. Robert Lloyd, whose grandmother Ella was a Purey-Cust and an aunt of Peggy, that we owe our thanks for his generous help answering questions and jogging the memory on many points about the Purey-Cust family in Lincolnshire.

(1)   John Betjeman *Summoned by Bells,* John Murray, London 1960, p25

Pedigree of a first love

(1)   Bevis Hillier, *Young Betjeman,* John Murray, London 1960, p20

(2)   GE Aylmer and Reginald Cant, *A History of York Minster,* Clarendon Press, Oxford 1977, p307

A Brief Betjeman Bibliography

A bibliography for inclusion in a book such as *Betjeman's Lincolnshire* must be, by necessity, brief and incomplete. It is intended to point the general reader in the direction of the main books which contain John Betjeman's verse, prose and letters, together with a number of biographical and critical studies.

For a more complete list, see *A Bibliographical Companion to Betjeman* (The Betjeman Society 1997) and *A Betjeman Checklist* (The Betjeman Society 2006) both compiled by Peter Gammond and John Heald.

John Betjeman's verse
Mount Zion (The James Press 1931) Facsimile reprint 1975
Continual Dew (John Murray 1937) Facsimile reprint 1977
Old Lights for New Chancels (John Murray 1940)
New Bats in Old Belfries (John Murray 1945)
Selected Poems (John Murray 1948)
A Few Late Chrysanthemums (John Murray 1954)
Poems in the Porch (SPCK 1954)
Collected Poems (John Murray 1958) – many reprints and updated editions since first publication. A centenary edition is planned for 2006.
Summoned by Bells (John Murray 1960)
High and Low (John Murray 1966)
A Nip in the Air (John Murray 1974)
The Best of Betjeman (John Murray in association with Penguin Books 1975)
Church Poems (John Murray 1981)
Uncollected Poems (John Murray 1982)

John Betjeman's Prose and Letters
Ghastly Good Taste (Chapman and Hall 1933) Revised and updated edition 1970 (Anthony Blond)
Cornwall – A Shell Guide (Architectural Press 1934) Revised and updated in 1964 (Faber)
Devon – A Shell Guide (Architectural Press 1936)
An Oxford University Chest (John Miles 1938) Reprinted 1979 (Oxford University Press)
Antiquarian Prejudice (Hogarth Press 1939)
Vintage London (Collins 1942)
English Cities and Small Towns (Collins 1943)
John Piper (Penguin Modern Painters 1944)
First and Last Loves (John Murray 1952)
Collins Guide to English Parish Churches (Collins 1958)
London's Historic Railway Stations (John Murray 1972)
A Pictorial History of English Architecture (John Murray 1972)
Archie and the Strict Baptists (John Murray 1977)
Letters Volume 1: 1926 – 1951, edited by Candida Lycett Green (Methuen 1994)
Letters Volume 2: 1951 - 1984, edited by Candida Lycett Green (Methuen 1995)

Coming Home, an anthology of prose, edited by Candida Lycett Green (Methuen 1997)

Biography

John Betjeman - A Study, Derek Stanford (Neville Spearman 1961)
John Betjeman – His Life and Work, Patrick Taylor-Martin (Allen Lane 1983)
John Betjeman – A Life in Pictures, Bevis Hillier (John Murray 1984)
Young Betjeman, Bevis Hillier (John Murray 1988)
John Betjeman, Dennis Brown, in the series Writers and their Work (Northcote House 1999)
John Betjeman – New Fame, New Love, Bevis Hillier (John Murray 2002)
Betjeman – The Bonus of Laughter, Bevis Hillier (John Murray 2004)

Subscribers

Name	Address
D Alexander	Hertford
Caroline Ashworth	Lastingham
TE Atkins	Windsor
Mrs J Attwood	Bury St Edmunds
Mr J Axon	Oakham
CM Barnes	Waddesdon
Robbie Barry	Godalming
Howard Baveystock	Alton
JSR Baxter	Canterbury
Mrs NJ Beechey	South Peverton
AG Bell	Cottingham
Larry Bennett	Lisvane
Ms S Bitterling	Clipsham
FW Blanchard	Fawley
DM Blood	Chesterfield
Mrs RM Bond	Peterborough
Richard Bowden	Westbury on Trym
AJ Branch	Harpenden
JG Britton	Toynton All Saints
Mrs WM Brooks	Coalville
Roy Burton	Didcot
Rodney Callow	Lincoln
David Campbell	Hornsey
Mrs S Carter	Skipton
CA Chase	Frinton on Sea
Robin Colyer	Ashby
Judith Cornish	Wrexham
John Cottenden	Chelsfield
Jennifer Coultan	Toynton All Saints
SE Crooks	Hagworthingham
Alan Dafforn	Middleton on Sea
Philippa Davies	Canterbury
Roy Denison	Reading
Richard Dennis	Kingston
Angie Dewick-Eisele	Alford
R Eden	Greenford
David Elliott	Horncastle
GK Faulkner	Louth
John Florance	Loughborough

L Fordham	Birchington
James Forrester	Hundleby
Jonathan Fryer	Sheerness
Peter Gammond	Shepperton
B & M Gibb-Gray	Emsworth
Mrs P Gibbs	Angmering
Judith Gilbert	Raithby
James Gilbert	Raithby
James Gilham	Egham
Mrs PM Godfrey	Searby
TE Goodman	Grantham
Susanna Gorst	Oxcombe
B Hacker	Tonbridge
Barbara Hale	Harpenden
David Hamilton	Ilford
Rev David Hare	Wymondham
Jane Hawkes	Woodhall Spa
Mr & Mrs Hazeldine	Waddington
John Heald	Guildford
John Hendy	Romney Marsh
Ralph Hentall	Hatfield
K Heywood	Deeping St James
KJ Hutton	Terrington St John
Steve Jackson	Chesterfield
Peter James	Kebworth Beauchamp
Gerry Jarvis	Macclesfield
Ian Jebbett	Sleaford
JK Jefferson	Skellingthorpe
Mrs Jane Kennedy	Llansoy
Mrs MM Kennedy	Leicester
Mrs D King	Spilsby
Barbara Kinnersley	Chesham
Clifford Knowles	Coleby
John Langford	Long Eaton
RM Lawie	Great Steeping
Kit Lawie	Toynton All Saints
Robin & Rachel Lawie	Brinkhill
D Lawrence	Grantham
Mr & Mrs G Leach	Bedford Park, London
Rita Learwood-Griffiths	Sutterton
DW Lee	Ardwick
Bruce Lewington	Aylesbury
Horace Liberty	Lincoln

Rodney Lines	Spalding
Marley R Lippiatt	St Davids
Rosemary Locke-Wheaton	Spilsby
Dr SJ Lucas	Cambridge
Mairi Macleod	Esher
Miss Maddison	Partney
IB Maw	Cottingham
Mrs B Maskell	Deeping St James
Beryl Middleton	Ashby
David Mitchell	Canterbury, NZ
Douglas Mitchell	Horncastle
Mrs D Mitchell-Smith	Hundleby
Baz & Sheila Morris	Narborough
Mrs MJ Morton	Miningsby
Stephen Mottram	Barnstaple
Anne & Robert Needham	Burgh on Bain
CJ Nickerson	Binbrook
M Norman	Sutton on Sea
Dawn O'Connor	East Keal
James Oxley-Brennan	Norwich
Hazel Parry	Chislehurst
Dr David Pattison	Oxford
Rev. Brian Peters	Sheffield
RM Pocock	Bracknell
Mrs P Powney	Clevedon
DWJ Price	Harrington
JS Reder	Rigsby
Mr & Mrs Renshaw	Spondon
Martin Revill	Bexley
David Richardson	Berkhamsted
G Richardson	Beverley
Michael & Ellen Richardson	East Keal
DN Robinson	Louth
Mrs A Rogers	Louth
Keith & Isabel Ross	Risley Hall
Jill Rundle	Alford
Christine Saffin	Woolston
Ruth Scarborough	Mavis Enderby
David & Margaret Sibley	Bingham
Maisie Sewards	Halton Holgate
Mrs DE Simpson	Southend on Sea

Mrs W Slaymaker	Oxford
Alan Smith	Ingoldmells
Jim Sterling	Kettering
Peter Taylor	Welton le Wold
Mrs G Taylor	Friskney
JS Taylor	Newark
Mark Temple	Woodhouse Eaves
J Thornalley	Alford
Elizabeth and Michael Thomas	Aby with Greenfield
John Timms	Bournemouth
Eileen Topliss	Rainworth
Philip Tremayne	Wallingford
R Treweek	Ingoldmells
Sylvia Trickett	Louth
Paul Walker	Dronfield
Ann Ward	Oakham
Mrs M Ward	Belchford
Gayne Wells	London
WM West	Sheffield
David Weston	Kirby Bellars
Mr & Mrs Wheeler	Market Harborough
David Williams	Wrexham
Catherine Wilson	Reepham
MJ Wilson	Hinkley
Raymond Woodfine	Weston
CN Wright	Allestree
Colin Wright	Shrewsbury
Denis & Margaret Wright	Sedgefield
MS & DE Wright	Spalding